Job   h
Hot   ls

D1417642

By Ron Krannich

CAREER AND BUSINESS BOOKS AND SOFTWARE

201 Dynamite Job Search Letters
America's Top 100 Jobs for People Without a Four-Year Degree
America's Top Jobs for People Re-Entering the Workforce
America's Top Internet Job Sites
Best Jobs for Ex-Offenders
Best Jobs for the 21st Century
Best Resumes and Letters for Ex-Offenders
Blue-Collar Resume and Job Hunting Guide
Change Your Job, Change Your Life
The Complete Guide to Public Employment
The Directory of Federal Jobs and Employers
The Educator's Guide to Alternative Jobs and Careers
The Ex-Offender's 30/30 Job Solutions
The Ex-Offender's Job Hunting Guide
The Ex-Offender's Job Interview Guide
The Ex-Offender's Quick Job Hunting Guide
The Ex-Offender's Re-Entry Success Guide
Find a Federal Job Fast!
From Army Green to Corporate Gray
Get a Raise in 7 Days
Give Me More Money!
High Impact Resumes and Letters
I Want to Do Something Else, But I'm Not Sure What It Is
Interview for Success
The Job Hunting Guide: Transitioning From College to Career
Job Hunting Tips for People With Hot and Not-So-Hot Backgrounds
Job Interview Tips for People With Not-So-Hot Backgrounds
Job-Power Source and *Ultimate Job Source* (software)
Jobs and Careers With Nonprofit Organizations
Military-to-Civilian Resumes and Letters
Military Transition to Civilian Success
Moving Out of Education
Moving Out of Government
Nail the Cover Letter!
Nail the Job Interview!
Nail the Resume!
No One Will Hire Me!
Overcoming Barriers to Employment
The Quick 30/30 Job Solution
Re-Careering in Turbulent Times
Re-Entry Employment and Life Skills Pocket Guide
Savvy Interviewing
The Savvy Networker
The Savvy Resume Writer
Win the Interview, Win the Job
You Should Hire Me!

TRAVEL AND INTERNATIONAL BOOKS

Best Resumes and CVs for International Jobs
The Complete Guide to International Jobs and Careers
The Directory of Websites for International Jobs
International Jobs Directory
Jobs for Travel Lovers
Politics of Family Planning Policy in Thailand
Shopping the Exotic South Pacific
Travel Planning On the Internet
Treasures and Pleasures of Australia
Treasures and Pleasures of Bermuda
Treasures and Pleasures of China
Treasures and Pleasures of Egypt
Treasures and Pleasures of Hong Kong
Treasures and Pleasures of India
Treasures and Pleasures of Indonesia
Treasures and Pleasures of Italy
Treasures and Pleasures of Mexico
Treasures and Pleasures of Paris and the French Riviera
Treasures and Pleasures of Rio and São Paulo
Treasures and Pleasures of Singapore and Bali
Treasures and Pleasures of Singapore and Malaysia
Treasures and Pleasures of Thailand and Myanmar
Treasures and Pleasures of Turkey
Treasures and Pleasures of Vietnam and Cambodia

Job Hunting Tips
for People with
Hot and Not-So-Hot
Backgrounds

2nd Edition

Ronald L. Krannich, Ph.D.

IMPACT PUBLICATIONS
Manassas Park, VA

Second Edition

ISBN: 978-1-57023-307-4 (13-digit); 1-57023-307-1 (10-digit)

Library of Congress: 2009934932

Publisher: For information on Impact Publications, including current and forthcoming publications, authors, press kits, online bookstore, and submission requirements, visit the left navigation bar on the front page of the publisher's main company website: www.impactpublications.com.

Publicity/Rights: For information on publicity, author interviews, and subsidiary rights, contact the Media Relations Department: Tel. 703-361-7300, Fax 703-335-9486, or email: query@impactpublications.com.

Sales/Distribution: All bookstore sales are handled through Impact's trade distributor: National Book Network, 15200 NBN Way, Blue Ridge Summit, PA 17214, Tel. 1-800-462-6420. All special sales and distribution inquiries should be directed to the publisher: Sales Department, IMPACT PUBLICATIONS, 9104 Manassas Drive, Suite N, Manassas Park, VA 20111-5211, Tel. 703-361-7300, Fax 703-335-9486, or email: query@impactpublications.com.

Publisher's Other Websites: www.exoffenderreentry.com, www.veteransworld.com, www.ishoparoundtheworld.com, www.greatwaterdestinations.com, www.middleeasttravellover.com

0 1021 0250880 5

Contents

Index to Tips

Key Job Search and Success Tips 7

Self-Assessment Tips 66

Goal and Objective Setting Tips 79

Research and Information Tips 88

Job Application Tips 104

Resume Writing, Distribution, and Follow-Up Tips 111

Cover and Job Search Letter Tips 139

Networking and Informational Interviewing Tips 147

Interviewing Tips **161**

Follow-Up and Follow-Through Tips 195

Salary Negotiation and Job Offer Tips . . 206

1

Expert Advice From the Job Search Trenches

INDING A JOB MAY BE THE hardest, most frustrating, and ego-bruising work you ever do if approached with a negative attitude. But there is a silver lining here. Indeed, job hunting can be an extremely educational, exciting, and exhilarating experience when viewed from a positive perspective. If done properly, you'll meet many new and interesting people, learn a great deal about yourself and others, and land a job that is a good fit for both you and the employer. You'll enjoy going to work each day where you can use your many gifts and talents. If all goes well, your new job will become an important step in your overall career. In the end, you'll be glad you approached this process with a positive attitude!

Job Hunting Tips for Everyone

Each year more than 30 million American actively conduct a job search. Another 30 million contemplate leaving their jobs for new opportunities elsewhere. While millions of people look for their first full-time job after leaving school, millions of others, including a large percentage who are in their first year of work, decide to quit their jobs because they are unhappy with their work. And millions of others get fired or laid off, re-enter the job market after a lengthy absence, decide to come out of retirement, take a second or third job, seek part-time work as students and homemakers, or transition from a different work world or lifestyle. In fact, each year nearly 250,000 individuals leave the military. While some retire, most look for new jobs and careers in the civilian work world. Each year over 650,000 ex-offenders seek employment upon release from prisons, jails, and detention centers. All of these individuals have one thing in common – they must conduct a job search that requires communicating their qualifications to strangers on applications and resumes as well as in job interviews.

Looking for a job is no fun, especially for the shy and sensitive who are forced to introduce themselves to **strangers**, ask for assistance, and encounter numerous rejections. Some people are immensely talented, very extroverted, and quickly find great jobs. Others are less talented, introverted, and find job hunting especially challenging and time consuming. These people may have great skills and experience, but they don't stand out from the crowd. Many other job seekers enter the job market with not-so-hot backgrounds that raise red flags in the eyes of employers who would prefer to distance themselves from what they see as potentially troublesome employees. While they may empathize, in the end few employers want to take the risks of giving troubled job seekers second, third, and fourth chances before they finally prove themselves capable with other employers.

> *Regardless of your background, you need to conduct a job search that best showcases your major strengths and talents to prospective employers.*

Whether you have a hot or not-so-hot background, you need to conduct a job search that best showcases and communicates your major strengths and talents to prospective employers. You need to do this right from the very start. Over the years I have learned numerous job hunting lessons from thousands of job seekers, employers, and career experts. Representing many occupations and walks of life, these individuals reveal a rich collection of job hunting tips that are equally applicable to people with hot and not-so-hot backgrounds. The tips constitute a set of principles for conducting an effective job search. By examining these tips, you should be able to better organize and target your job search, lessen your anxiety, and go on to land a job that best fits your interests, skills, and abilities. Better still, you should be able to substantially shorten your job search time. In so doing, these tips will both save and earn you a great deal of money!

You're Under Suspicion

Finding a job is especially challenging if you have red flags in your background and feel the need to cover up, shade the truth, or lie about your past. If, for example, you've been fired, incarcerated, lack appropriate skills and education, received poor grades, offer weak or negative references, appear to be a job hopper, seem overqualified, remain unfocused, have medical or disability issues, or experienced a divorce or bankruptcy, you need to be prepared to deal with these negatives during your job search, especially when completing applications and being interviewed for a job.

Here is the sobering situation you are likely to encounter these days: employers are suspicious of most candidates who come to them as strangers. You are asking them to give you a position, salary, and benefits in exchange for the promise of

In today's high-tech, security-conscious, and behavior-oriented society, there is no place to hide!

performance. In the past, they have had experiences with candidates who exaggerated their qualifications, lied on their resumes, and performed far below expectations. Trusting the information provided by the candidate, they eventually felt deceived when they had to deal with the realities of day-to-day performance.

Not surprisingly, employers want better control of the hiring process. They want to more accurately predict an individual's future performance based on an accurate assessment of their **past accomplishments**. As employers increasingly screen candidates through background checks, testing, references, and situational interviews, fewer prospective employees can avoid the close scrutiny that often reveals red flags in their backgrounds. Indeed, in today's high-tech, security-conscious, and behavior-oriented society, there is no place to hide! Employers want to know your work history and related patterns of behavior – both positives and negatives – that they may inherit.

If you have red flags in your background, chances are they will follow you throughout your job search as well as on the job and in your life. Therefore, you should be prepared to deal with red flags that may become potential job knock-outs. You'll need to have a thorough understanding of the job search process and how you can best deal with red flags at each stage in your job search.

The "No One Will Hire Me!" Lament

Over the years I have worked with numerous people who frequently lamented what they considered to be a fact of job search life – *"No one will hire me!"* After spending weeks looking for a job, they encountered numerous rejections and thus concluded there were few jobs available for people with their qualifications. On closer examination, however, I found that much of the problem in finding employment related to the individual rather than the job market. Many of these people spent most of their job search time responding to classified ads in newspapers and job postings on the Internet – the least effective ways of finding a job. Regardless of their stellar or not-so-stellar backgrounds, most of them made several job search mistakes that knocked them out of the competition. These mistakes include:

- Harbor negative and self-defeating "can't do" attitudes
- Lack clear goals and a work objective
- Misunderstand the sequential nature of a job search
- Engage in several ineffective job search activities
- Fail to network, or network with the wrong people
- Provide little evidence of skills, accomplishments, and a productive pattern of behavior
- Write and distribute awful resumes and letters
- Include negative or incomplete information on applications
- Commit several job interview sins, from arriving late to failing to close the interview properly
- Fail to ask questions, listen, and make modifications
- Lack tactfulness and honesty
- Conduct an outdated job search
- Over-rely on technology, especially the Internet
- Avoid taking risks

- Unprepared to handle rejections
- Fail to develop and implement a plan of action
- Exhibit weak follow-up skills
- Try to conduct a job search on their own rather than seek professional help at critical steps in their job search
- Resist changing behaviors and acquiring new habits
- Fail to keep motivated throughout the job search

Taken together, these mistakes project an unflattering image of the candidate – someone who is not quite up to doing the job. If you add to this list any red flags in your background, you may have a powerful set of factors working against your best interests. Indeed, your success in finding a good job may be limited by your inability to clearly communicate your positive qualifications to prospective employers.

My Mission

My primary goal in writing this book is to bring together some of the best advice from job seekers, employers, and career professionals on how to find a job. While some of my tips may appear obvious, most are not. From assessing skills, conducting research, and writing

> *Based on key job search principles, my tips are actually a comprehensive guide to success in today's job market.*

resumes to networking, interviewing, and negotiating salaries, these tips are based on solid principles of job search success.

One of my purposes in writing this book also is to provide assistance to millions of job seekers who have red flags in their backgrounds. This is a very large but much neglected group of job seekers. Take, for example, a set of very revealing statistics. Approximately 50 million Americans have some type of conviction on their record. While over 650,000 ex-offenders are released from prisons each year, approximately 70 percent will become incarcerated again sometime within the first three years of release. This high recidivism rate is largely attributed to the failure of ex-offenders to find meaningful employment. Many receive $50 in gate money upon release, but they have no idea of what they are going to do to find employment. As a result, many return to their former dysfunctional neighborhoods, friends, and families and then repeat a similar behavioral pattern that was responsible for their incarceration in the first place. Other not-so-hot backgrounds may result from a pattern of job hopping, having been fired, lacking appropriate education and training, and dealing with persistent financial and personal problems that impact on one's work life.

Like most job seekers, these individuals have skills and abilities sought by employers. But what separates them from other candidates is their not-so-hot background. A background check may quickly reveal a set of behaviors that raise red flags in the minds of potential employers who are reluctant to hire such "risky" people.

At the same time, people with not-so-hot backgrounds encounter similar job search problems encountered by individuals with stellar backgrounds, especially goal setting, negative attitudes, rejections, awful resumes, and dreadful interview performance. In the following pages I outline a combination of job hunting tips that relate to people with not-so-hot backgrounds as well as those that affect the job search process in general, regardless of your background.

Useful Tips and Principles for Success

As you will quickly discover in Tip #2 of Chapter 2, this book is organized around a well defined seven-step sequential job search process. While the next chapter deals with many key aspects of the job search, all subsequent chapters include a set of tips that focus on a particular job search step, such as self-assessment and goal setting, research, resumes and cover letters, networking, and interviewing. After completing all of these chapters, you should have a thorough understanding of how to conduct an effective job search based upon a clear understanding of all the components that define effectiveness.

I wish you well as you embark on this new adventure. Whether you have a hot or not-so-hot background, you will at least be armed with a set of useful tips and principles that will help you land a great new job. Better still, with the right attitude toward learning, you may actually find your job search can be a great deal of fun as you begin meeting talented people and developing new networks of supportive relationships! Whatever you do, approach your job search with a **positive attitude** that will serve you well in finding a great new job!

2

Key Job Search and Success Tips

THE 37 TIPS IN THIS chapter debunk popular beliefs about how best to find a job. Best of all, they help you organize a well targeted job search over a specific time period. In many respects, these are the most basic tips for launching an effective job search, regardless of your background. They will give you the "big picture" (the forest) before you engage in many specific activities (the trees) from which you may lose perspective on what you should be doing when conducting an effective job search.

TIP #1
Make your job search a top priority activity.

If you are serious about finding a good job, you simply must make your job search a top priority activity. Too often job seekers engage in a great deal of wishful thinking. They speculate about the ideal type of work they might be doing, how much more money they will make, and the new benefits they will receive. However, many such dreamers don't do enough to make things happen. They continue their normal daily routines, allowing little time to engage in the many critical and time- consuming activities that make up an effective job search, such as conducting research, making telephone calls, writing resumes and letters, and networking. It should be the first and last thing you think about during the day. You make your job search a top priority by putting it at the very top of your daily "to do" list. Indeed, the first three items on your 10-item "to do" list should relate to your job search. For example, your daily list may look this:

> *Put your job search at the very top of your daily "to do" list.*

1. Investigate job openings with two local department stores.
2. Contact three people on my networking list for referrals.
3. Write three thank-you letters for referrals.
4. Call Tim about meeting on Friday.
5. Contact Mary for dinner on Saturday.
6. Meet with Diana at 3:30pm.
7. Pick up cleaning.
8. Stop at grocery store.
9. Reschedule dental appointment for next Tuesday.
10. Call Dave about lawn problem.

If you always put your job search activities at the top of your list, you will force yourself to make your job search a daily priority. To do less than this is not to take your job search and your future very seriously – you're engaged in wishful thinking.

TIP #2
Organize your job search as a seven-step sequential process.

As illustrated on page 9, your job search should be organized as a seven-step process. Each step should be followed in sequence. For example, the very first step of any job search should involve a self-assessment through which you (1) identify your motivated abilities and skills and (2) specify a job or career objective. These first two activities are the foundation steps for effectively completing all other

Job Search Steps and Stages

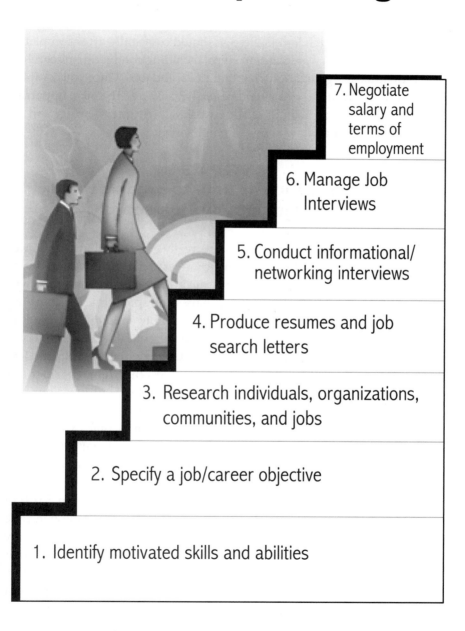

7. Negotiate salary and terms of employment

6. Manage Job Interviews

5. Conduct informational/ networking interviews

4. Produce resumes and job search letters

3. Research individuals, organizations, communities, and jobs

2. Specify a job/career objective

1. Identify motivated skills and abilities

job search steps. While many job seekers begin by writing a resume without having assessed their interests, skills, and abilities and formulated an objective, they often create resumes that do not clearly communicate what they have done, can do, and want to do. Writing resumes and job search letters, Step 4, should come only **after** completing three preliminary preparation steps, including conducting research on individuals, organizations, communities, and jobs. Once you complete a powerful resume, you should be ready to execute the most important steps in your job search – (5) networking, (6) interviewing, and (7) negotiating salary and terms of employment.

TIP #3
Take sufficient time to organize and implement your job search.

Anyone can find a job, but finding a really good job that you do well and enjoy doing will involve a major investment of your time. If you are a busy person who feels you have little spare time for anything, you simply **must** find time to conduct your job search. If you don't think you can find sufficient time to do this right, consider this fact of employment life: Your new job could be worth an additional $1 million in income over the next several years, especially if you land a job that pays substantially more than your past or current job. So just how much is your time worth? $5, $10, $25, $50, or $100 an hour. If every hour you invest in your job search results in $100 of additional income, you may decide you can indeed find enough time to conduct a serious job search. Start by analyzing how you currently use your time. Most people, for example, spend 80 percent of their time on self-absorbed trivia – do you Twitter and play with your email, iPod, BlackBerry, and online social networks a lot? – and 20 percent on things that really matter. You need to reverse those percentages so that 80 percent of your time is used effectively. Start reorganizing your time by addressing a few basic time management questions:

> *Most people spend 80 percent of their time on trivia and 20 percent of their time on things that really matter.*

- Do you know how to say "no" or do you tend to say "yes" to everything?

- Do you place a dollar value on your time and act accordingly?

- Do you let others control your time or do you take charge of your time?

- Do you quickly dispense with your junk mail and email or do your ponder and save it?

- Do you spend a great deal of time engaged in online activities that may well be an addiction to electronic trivia?

- Do you set priorities, use a scheduling calendar, and set work targets?

Chances are you can find time for your job search if you first reassess how you currently use your time. Finding a job can take as little as a few days or as long as six months to one year, depending on how you organize and implement your job search. Most job seekers take from three to six months to find a job in today's job market. As indicated in the hypothetical chart on page 12, each of the sequential job search steps outlined on page 9 occur over

> *Most job seekers take from three to six months to find a job in today's job market.*

a six-month period. Depending on a combination of good planning, serendipity, and luck, job interviews and offers can occur at any time. You can accelerate this time line by spending more time on your job search. If, for example, you only devote 10 hours a week to finding a job, chances are it will take you a long time to connect with the right job. However, if you make this a full-time endeavor by spending 40 to 80 hours a week engaged in various job search activities, you may be able to shorten your job search time from three months to one month. Your success in finding a job will depend on how much time and effort you devote to your search. Whatever you do, do not get discouraged and give up prematurely after encountering only a few rejections (see

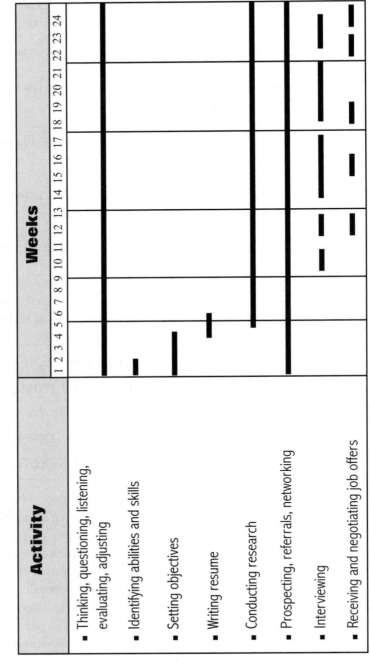

Organization of Job Search Activities

Tip #24). Keeping focused on completing and repeating each job search activity over a 24-week time line will eventually pay off with a job that's right for you. You can even substantially accelerate this process by engaging in a full arsenal of unconventional guerrilla job search activities that will nearly guarantee that you find a job within 30 days and within 30 miles of your home. Neil McNulty and I outline how to do this in our book *The Quick 30/30 Job Solution: Smart Job Search Tips for Surviving Today's New Economy.*

TIP #4
Commit yourself in writing by signing a job search contract and completing weekly performance and planning reports.

You must keep focused, motivated, and committed throughout your job search. It's not surprising that the single most important impediment to conducting a successful job search is the **failure to implement**. While you can have all the dreams, plans, and positive thinking you want, if you don't translate those dreams, plans, and thinking into daily and weekly plans of action, you will be going nowhere with your job search. Based on your self-assessment activities (Step 1), you need to specify how your objective (Step 2) will translate into research, resume and letter writing, and networking activities (Steps 3-5). One of the best ways to do this is to commit yourself in writing by completing the Job Search Contract and Weekly Job Performance and Planning Report on pages 14 and 15. This contract and report will serve as key documents for both prioritizing and implementing your job search as well as keeping you focused and motivated on what you need to do in order to conduct a successful job search.

TIP #5
Approach your job search for positive rather than negative reasons.

Attitude, optimism, and enthusiasm are very important when looking for a job. They will help you handle the many psychological ups and downs you are likely to encounter when looking for a job.

Job Search Contract

1. I'm committed to changing my life by changing my job. Today's date is _____.

2. I will manage my time so that I can successfully complete my job search and find a high quality job. I will begin changing my time management behavior on _____.

3. I will begin my job search on _____.

4. I will involve _____ with my job search.
   (individual/group)

5. I will spend at least one week conducting library research on different jobs, employers, and organizations. I will begin this research during the week of _____.

6. I will complete my skills identification step by _____.

7. I will complete my objective statement by _____.

8. I will complete my resume by _____.

9. Each week I will:

   - make _____ new job contacts.

   - conduct _____ informational interviews.

   - follow up on _____ referrals.

10. My first job interview will take place during the week of _____.

11. I will begin my new job by _____.

12. I will make a habit of learning one new skill each year.

Signature: _____

Date: _____

Weekly Job Performance and Planning Report

1. The week of: _____.

2. This week I:

   - wrote ____ job search letters.
   - sent ____ resumes and ____ letters to potential employers.
   - completed ____ applications.
   - made ____ job search telephone calls.
   - completed ____ hours of job research.
   - set up ____ appointments for informational interviews.
   - conducted ____ informational interviews.
   - received ____ invitations to a job interview.
   - followed up on ____ contacts and ____ referrals.

3. Next week I will:

   - write ____ job search letters.
   - send ____ resumes and ____ letters to potential employers.
   - complete ____ applications.
   - make ____ job search telephone calls.
   - complete ____ hours of job research.
   - set up ____ appointments for informational interviews.
   - conduct ____ informational interviews.
   - follow up on ____ contacts and ____ referrals.

4. Summary of progress this week in reference to my Job Search Contract commitments:

   _____
   _____
   _____
   _____
   _____
   _____

If you lost your job or seek a new job because you are unhappy with your current job, chances are you may be approaching your job search for negative reasons. Perhaps you may feel unjustly fired or you dislike your boss or co-workers. Such feelings can be translated into negative attitudes that get communicated to prospective employers. Always keep in mind that employers want to hire positive, energetic, and enthusiastic individuals who also are likely to be intelligent and show initiative. They don't want to hire negative people or those who have an attitude problem or seem to dislike their work. If you have negative reasons for seeking a job, you probably need to improve your attitude. Start by listing eight reasons why you are looking for a job:

1. _____

2. _____

3. _____

4. _____

5. _____

6. _____

7. _____

8. _____

Review your list and cross out any negative reasons for seeking a new job. Replace the negative statements with a restatement of the negative reason in a positive way, or with additional positive reasons. Now, rank order all eight statements with "1" representing the most important positive reason for seeking a new job.

You also should examine your language when talking about your past, present, and future employment. Everything you include on your resume and in your job search letters should be **employer-centered** and emphasize the **positive**, starting with your **objective**. During job interviews, avoid using words and phrases that might indicate possible negative attitudes or questionable motivations. Common negatives such as *"didn't," "wouldn't," "can't,"* and *"don't"* often communicate the wrong messages to employers:

Negative	**Positive**
I *didn't* get a raise.	I expected my performance would be better rewarded.
I *wouldn't* take that assignment in Buffalo.	I love this community and want to stay here for many years.
I *can't* afford a car right now.	Transportation should be no problem.
I *don't* know how to operate that program.	I would love to learn how to operate that program.

If asked why you left your previous job, don't talk about negative experiences, disappointments, or history, such as the fact that you didn't like your boss, you were passed over for a promotion, you were fired, or you just didn't like working for jerks. While these may be legitimate reasons for leaving and you are being frank and honest, such negative reasons communicate the wrong messages and attitudes to prospective employers who are interested in hiring your

Your positive attitude may become your most important asset throughout your job search.

future rather than inheriting your past. Instead, focus on the positive and the future by talking about your past accomplishments and your interest in seeking new opportunities and more fully utilizing your skills.

If you keep a positive attitude and focus on the positive – what's right about you, the job, and the employer – you'll quickly discover this positive approach will be contagious. It will help motivate you, keep your morale up despite rejections, and communicate optimism and enthusiasm to those around you. Indeed, your positive attitude may become your most important asset throughout your job search.

TIP #6
Don't spend a great deal of time looking for jobs in newspapers or on the Internet.

Most job seekers spend a great deal of time looking for and responding to job vacancies in the classified section of newspapers and on employment websites. They send resumes and letters in response to such listings in the hope of being called for a job interview. Such activities give job seekers a false sense of making progress in the job market, because they believe they are doing something they think will result in a job. These also are the main job search activities of many frustrated job seekers who complain there no jobs available for them or that employers are not interested in hiring them. I hear this complaint again and again from job seekers who are primarily focused on finding employment through newspapers and the Internet. But the likelihood of landing a job this way is similar to being struck by lightning – very unlikely. In fact, these are the least effective places to look for employment. Known as the "advertised job market," because employers pay to have their job vacancies listed in these media, only about 15 percent of individuals find jobs through these channels. Research continues to confirm that most jobs – over 80 percent – are found on the "hidden job market." These jobs are found through word-of-mouth, networking, cold calls, knocking on doors, and direct application. Jobs found on the hidden job market also tend to be better paying, more secure, less competitive, higher quality, and more satisfying than those found on the advertised job market. Advertised jobs are disproportionately competitive, difficult to fill, and low-paying positions. After all, employers often have to advertise a job because they find it is difficult to fill through other less public means.

> *Over 80 percent of all jobs are found on the "hidden job market." Only 15 percent of jobs are found on the "advertised job market."*

TIP #7
Learn to find jobs on the hidden job market.

As we noted in Tip #6, you should spend most of your job search time focused on the hidden job market. If you spend more than 30 percent of your time looking for jobs through classified ads and on the Internet, you are most likely wasting a great deal of job search time that could be put to more productive use by engaging in the most effective job search activities, especially cold-calling, networking, and informational interviews.

Periodically check what percent of your time is spent on the advertised job market. If you discover you are spending more than 30 percent of your time engaged in this market, reorganize your job search so that it is focused on more effective activities. Your goal should be to get as many job interviews as possible – not to send out lots of resumes and letters in the hope of connecting to a few employers. As you will see once we examine effective networking strategies, the fastest way to get job interviews is through networking for information, advice, and referrals.

Individuals with not-so-hot backgrounds should spend most of their job search time focused on the hidden job market. Networking and cold-calling activities enable them to be pre-screened by many individuals who will refer them to employers interested in their abilities and skills. Employers found on the hidden job market are less likely to rely on paper qualifications, which often accentuate red flags of applicants with difficult backgrounds. Through networking, you are screened more on the basis of face-to-face meetings and conversations, where what you say and do during the encounters are more important than what you have written in your resume, letters, and applications.

TIP #8
Use the Internet to research jobs and employers, acquire career advice, and communicate by email.

Few job seekers know how to use the Internet properly in their job search. A very seductive medium, the Internet holds more promise than performance when it comes to finding a job. Unfortunately, a disproportionate number of job seekers use the Internet to find employment, believing that employers actually hire over the Internet! Such job seekers spend an inordinate amount of time posting their resume to popular job sites, such as Monster.com, HotJobs.Yahoo. com, and CareerBuilder.com, and responding to job listings in the hopes of being struck by lightning! Research continues to show that less than 20 percent of job seekers found their last job by engaging in such online activities that eventually led to job interviews and an offer.

The Internet is a wonderful information and communication tool that is best used, in a job search, for (1) conducting research on jobs, employers, companies, and communities; (2) acquiring useful advice and referrals; and (3) communicating with individuals via email. Indeed, your most productive online activities will relate to research and communication. While you should post your resume on various employment websites and periodically review online job listings, just don't spend a great deal of time doing so and then waiting to hear from employers based on such activities. Move on to other more productive activities, especially visiting employer websites, which are more likely to yield useful information, job listings, and applications than the more general and popular employment websites. In fact, since more and more employers recruit directly from their own websites, rather than use general employment websites, you are well advised to explore employer websites for employment information. For example, companies such as Microsoft (www.microsoft.com/careers) and Boston Consulting Group (www.bcg.com) provide a wealth of information for job seekers interested in their companies. You can learn a great deal about job hunting by visiting those two websites alone. But your most useful online job search activity relates to **research**. Thousands of websites can yield useful information for enhancing your job search. For example, use the Internet to explore different jobs (www.bls.gov/ oco) and employers (www.hoovers.com), community-based employment assistance (www. careeronestop.org), career counselors (www.nbcc.org), networking groups (www.linkedin.com), salary ranges (www.salary.com), best communities (www.findyourspot.com), relocation (www.homefair.com),

> *Your most productive online activities will relate to research and communication.*

and career advice (www.wetfeet.com). You can even use the Internet to conduct an online assessment (www.careerlab.com), blast your resume to thousands of employers (www.resumeblaster.com), contact recruiters (www.recruitersonline.com), and explore hundreds of professional associations (www.ipl.org/div/aon) and nonprofit organizations (www.guidestar.org) that are linked to thousands of employers.

For more information on how to wisely use the Internet in your job search, see *America's Top Internet Job Sites*, *Job Hunting Online*, and *Guide to Internet Job Searching*, which are available through Impact Publications (www.impactpublications.com or see the order form at the end of this book).

TIP #9
Treat your job search as a people process rather than a paper and email exercise.

In the end, people hire **people**. Resumes, letters, and applications are **screening devices**. Employers hire individuals based upon the outcome of face-to-face interviews rather than on the content of their written communications. Therefore, the purpose of your paper, pencil, and typing activities is to make **connections** with the right people who, in turn, will invite you to a job interview based upon the quality of your written communication and possibly a telephone screening interview. Whatever you do, make sure your paper and email products are perfect –

Make sure your paper and email products are perfect – error-free and well targeted – since they represent your best efforts to strangers.

error-free and well targeted – since they represent your best efforts to strangers whom you need to persuade to invite you to a job interview. The whole networking process, which is the basis for finding the best quality jobs, is primarily a people process – you connect to other individuals by way of telephone calls and face-to-face meetings. How you communicate both verbally and nonverbally will largely determine the outcome of your job search. Be especially attentive to what you say and do when networking and interviewing for a job.

TIP #10
Apply for jobs that match your qualifications.

Many job seekers engage in a great deal of random and wishful thinking activities, such as applying for jobs that have little relationship to their qualifications. When employers look for employees, they are trying to solve specific problems relating to skills and experience they need. They usually know exactly what they want in terms of qualifications and spell their needs out accordingly. Don't waste your time applying for jobs for which you are not qualified or ones for which you're greatly over-qualified. Try to match your qualifications as closely as possible with the requirements of the job. One of the most effective ways to do this to create a "T" letter that clearly states how your qualifications match the specific requirements for the job. Take, for example, the "T" letter on page 23, which can be used in lieu of a resume when applying for a position. This letter emphasizes a one-to-one match between the employer's job requirements and the candidate's qualifications. Employers who receive such letters have little difficulty screening a candidate's qualifications since they are spelled our in the clearest terms possible. Employers usually respond well to such letters since they do not need to spend a great deal of time interpreting a general resume, letter, or application that may be written for many types of employers. Be specific, be targeted, and be responsive whenever you respond to job vacancy announcements.

> *Create a "T" letter that clearly states how your qualifications match the specific requirements for the job.*

TIP #11
Choose your language carefully – it should communicate energy and enthusiasm and command the attention of others.

Employers want to hire energetic and enthusiastic people. Such people have a positive attitude about their job, work, and future. They tend

"T" Letter

July 21, 20 ___

Darlene Compton
Timberlake-Thompson Company
892 Champion Drive
Austin, TX 77889

Dear Ms. Compton:

I'm responding to your job posting that appears on the CareerCenter website for a Public Relations Specialist. My profile is available online (#1234321) with CCC and I e-mailed a copy of my resume to you today as you requested.

I believe I am an excellent candidate for this position given my interests, educational background, and recent internship experience in PR:

Your Requirements	**My Qualifications**
1+ years of experience in PR	Served as a PR intern during the past three summers; focused on sales and marketing strategies.
Strong interpersonal skills	Praised by professors and supervisors for working well in teams and with both co-workers and clients. Received the "Intern of the Year" Award in 2006.
Ability to develop compelling ad copy	Developed copy for three ad campaigns which were used in major media spots. Client realized a 30% increase in sales due to these efforts.
Energetic and willing to travel	Work well with deadlines and stressful situations. "Energy and enthusiasm" cited as major characteristics in receiving the internship award. Love to travel.

In addition, I know the importance of building strong customer relations and developing innovative approaches to today's new PR mediums. I love taking on new challenges, working in multiple team and project settings, and seeing clients achieve results from my company's efforts.

I believe there is a strong match between your needs and my professional interests and qualifications. Could we meet soon to discuss how we might best work together? I'll call your office Tuesday at 11am to see if your schedule might permit such a meeting.

I appreciate your consideration and looking forward to speaking with you on Tuesday.

Sincerely,

Sterling Richards

Sterling Richards

to be productive people who work well with others. Despite occasional ups and downs, make sure you maintain a positive attitude throughout your job search as well as on the job. Accept rejections as part of the job search. Be persistent and continue to move on expecting you will encounter acceptances.

While your resume and applications generally follow a standard format for presenting qualifications, your job search letters and email provide opportunities for you to express your personality. Choose language that expresses a positive attitude, energy, and enthusiasm. You can **energize** your resume and job search letters by using action verbs and the active voice. Avoid the passive voice, which tends to remove you from action and make you sound less than enthusiastic. If your grammar rules are a bit rusty, here are some examples of action verbs:

> *Create a "T" letter that clearly states how your qualifications match the specific requirements for the job.*

administered	investigated
analyzed	managed
assisted	negotiated
communicated	organized
conducted	planned
coordinated	proposed
created	recommended
designed	recruited
developed	reduced
directed	reorganized
established	revised
evaluated	selected
expanded	streamlined
generated	supervised
implemented	trained
increased	trimmed
initiated	wrote

When applied to the active voice, action or transitive verbs follow a particular grammatical pattern:

Subject	Action Verb	Direct Object
I	increased	profits
I	initiated	studies
I	expanded	production

However, omit the subject (I) if listing your accomplishments. If written in the passive voice versus the active voice, compare how these examples would appear in the "Experience" section of a resume in the following form:

Passive Voice	Active Voice
Profits were increased by 32 percent.	Increased profits by 32 percent.
The studies resulted in new legislation.	Initiated studies that resulted in new legislation.
Production was expanded by 24 percent.	Expanded production by 24 percent.

Which one sounds better and makes you appear more action-oriented? It's obvious – the active voice. Avoid using the passive voice since it diminishes your value. With the passive voice, readers aren't sure what you did versus what others in your company or organization did. If you use action verbs and the active voice, you can clearly write about **your** accomplishments and inject energy into your writing. Action verbs imply that you, the subject, performed the action. The reader will know **you** were in charge and got things done.

When you inject energy, enthusiasm, and personality into your writing, you inform the reader that you are not the typical job seeker who is going through the mechanics of applying for a job. Contrast, for example, these two job search letters which are important in a networking campaign for generating informational interviews:

Letter #1

Janice Walker recommended that I write to you concerning my interest in landscape architecture. I would appreciate an opportunity to discuss possible job opportunities for someone with my background. I'm enclosing my resume for your reference. I look forward to hearing from you.

Letter #2

Janice Walker was right. Your work at Meadows Fields was brilliant. I know because I closely watched the landscape changes that took place there when I was working for R.C. Associates. In fact, borrowing from your innovative retainer wall design that incorporated the use of both stone and timber materials, we were able to develop an award-winning design for the new Jenkins Park on Olivia Reservoir. I also was able to develop a series of attractive ponds and fountains that quickly became models for several commercial projects. I'm excited about the possibility of doing similar work with a company that would be interested in my unique approach to several architectural elements which I've developed over the past six months. Could we meet? I will call you Tuesday morning.

Which letter appeals to you more? While both of these approach letters begin with a personal connection to Janice Walker, the remainder of the letters are quite different. The first letter is the typical formal letter of introduction most job seekers write. It's basically a throw-away. It tells you nothing about the writer other than his asking for the recipient's help in his job search – perhaps obligatory (because of a personal connection) but time-consuming encounter that most people would like to avoid. The second letter is different and stands out as special. It speaks directly to the interests of the recipient. Best of all, it expresses a genuine sense of energy and enthusiasm. Chances are the reader will be impressed with the second letter, which appears to be written by a very interesting and talented individual, and may actually want to meet with the writer.

Words such as "delighted," "excited," "happy," "enjoy," and "look forward" tend to communicate a positive attitude. Talking about skills, accomplishments, and performance emphasizes action and outcomes. Whether you are writing, talking over the telephone, or in a face-to-face interview, choose words and phrases that emphasize your energy and enthusiasm. For excellent compendiums of positive keywords and phrases to use in your job search, see Wendy S. Enelow's two books – *Best KeyWords for Resumes, Cover Letters, and Interviews* and *KeyWords to Nail Your Job Interview* (Impact Publications) – which are available through the order form at the end of this book.

TIP #12
Don't assume too much about employers and the competition.

Job seekers hold many questionable beliefs about employers and the job market. Two of the biggest myths are these:

1. Employers are in the driver's seat.

2. Employers hire the best qualified candidates.

In reality, most employers are not in the driver's seat, because they are trying to solve a hiring problem and thus must rely on an unpredictable job market for a solution. While some employers are very good at identifying their hiring needs, screening applicants, and selecting the best candidate, other employers lack hiring expertise. Some employers don't have a clear idea of the specific skills and experience they need, and do a poor job of screening candidates. Since many employers lack good interviewing skills and inside knowledge

> *Few employers hire the best qualified candidates. They select someone they like and who is currently available for employment.*

about their competition, especially relating to salaries and benefits, few employers actually hire the best qualified candidates. Rather, through a very imperfect hiring process, they select someone they like and who is currently available for employment. Furthermore, few employers actually subject candidates to the most effective screening techniques – behavioral and situational interviews and thorough background checks concerning actual job performance – for determining the best qualified candidates. Knowing this, job seekers can help employers define their needs in terms of the job seeker's qualifications. Those who know how to best communicate their qualifications, energy, and enthusiasm to employers are in a good position to persuade employers to hire them over what is often weak competition. Therefore, if you organize an intelligent job search and target employers accordingly, you may actually be in the driver's seat!

TIP #13
Seek professional help if necessary – don't play Lone Ranger all the time.

Many job seekers believe they can conduct a job search on their own. Just write a resume and send it to several employers. Within a few days their phone should start ringing and they will be interviewed and offered a job.

Fewer than 20 percent of all job seekers can effectively conduct a job search on their own. Most could benefit from working with others.

In reality, the job search is much more complicated and unpredictable. While a resume is important for presenting qualifications to employers, the job interview is by far the most important element to landing a job. No resume, no interview; no interview, no job offer.

At the same time, it may take three to six months to find the right job. During that time, most job seekers encounter numerous disheartening rejections that often diminish their energy and enthusiasm. My experience is that fewer than 20 percent of all job seekers can effectively conduct a job search on their own just by following the advice of career experts. The successful individuals tend to be self-starters who are very focused and motivated. The remaining 80 percent of job seekers can benefit from some form of assistance from career counselors, coaches, or a support group. Having someone to work with and share your experience with, including the inevitable ups and downs, can help immensely in moving your job search ahead. In fact, many job seekers can cut their job search time in half by working with a professional or support group. A career professional can be especially helpful at certain critical stages of your job search, especially in conducting a self-assessment, writing resumes, and preparing for interviews.

Starting on the next page are some of the most important sources and services for acquiring professional assistance. Each of these services has certain advantages and disadvantages. Approach them with caution. Since career planning is a big and largely unregulated business, you will occasionally encounter hucksters and fraudulent services aimed at taking advantage of individuals who are psychologically vulnerable and naive. Many of these hucksters self-certify themselves, promise to locate jobs that pay more than your last one, and seal the deal by ask ing for up-front money – $500 to $15,000 – to find you a job. Lacking good shopping sense and engaging in wishful thinking, many job seekers fall for the false promises of these so-called employment experts.

*When shopping for a career professional, never sign a contract before you read the fine print, get a second opinion, and talk to former clients about **results**.*

Our advice is very simple: **Never** sign a contract before you read the fine print, get a second opinion, and talk to former clients about the **results** they achieved through the service. While most of these services are not free, there is no reason to believe that the most expensive services are the best services. In fact, you may get the same quality of services from a group that charges $300 versus one that costs much more. At the same time, free or cheap services are not necessarily as good as the more expensive services. While you often get what you pay for in this industry, you also may get much less than what you pay for. Again, before using any employment services or hiring an expert, do your research by asking for references and contacting individuals who have used the services.

With these words of caution in mind, let's examine a variety of services available, some of which you may want to incorporate in your career planning and job search efforts.

1. Public employment services

Public employment services usually consist of a state agency which provides employment assistance as well as pays unemployment compensation benefits. Employment assistance largely consists of job listings and counseling services. However, counseling services often screen individuals for employers who list with the public employment agency. If you are looking for an entry-level job or a job paying $18,000 to $40,000, contact these services. However, most employers still do not list with them, especially for positions paying more than $40,000 a year.

Although the main purpose of these offices has been to dispense unemployment benefits, don't overlook them because of past stereotypes. The Workforce Development Act has re-energized such services. Within the past decade, many of these offices have literally "reinvented" themselves for today's new job market as One-Stop Career Centers (www.careeronestop.org), offering computerized job banks, counseling services, training programs, and other innovative organizational and technical approaches. Many of them offer useful employment services, including self-assessment and job search workshops as well as access to job listings on the Internet. Most of these offices are linked to U.S. Department of Labor's three useful websites – Job Bank Information www.jobbankinfo.org, America's Career InfoNet (www.acinet.org), and CareerOneStop (www.careerone stop.org). If you are a veteran, you will find many of the jobs listed with state employment offices give veterans preference in hiring. Go see for yourself if your state employment office offers useful services for you.

2. Private employment agencies

Private employment agencies work for money, either from applicants or employers. Approximately 8,000 such agencies operate nationwide. Many are highly specialized in technical, scientific, and financial fields. The majority of these firms serve the interests of employers, since employers – not applicants – represent repeat business. While employers normally pay the placement fee, many agencies charge applicants 10 to 15 percent of their first-year salary. These firms have one major advantage: job leads which you may have difficulty uncovering elsewhere. Especially for highly specialized fields, a good firm can be extremely helpful. The major disadvantages are that they can be costly and the quality of the firms varies. Be careful in how you deal with them. Make sure you understand the fee structure and what they will do for you before you sign anything.

3. **Temporary staffing firms**

During the past decade temporary staffing firms have come of age as more and more employers turn to them for recruitment assistance. They offer a variety of employment services to both applicants and employers who are either looking for temporary work and workers or who want to better screen applicants and employers. Many of these temp firms, such as Manpower (www.manpower.com), Olsten (www.olsten.com), and Kelly Services (www.kellyservices.com), recruit individuals for a wide range of positions and skill levels as well as full-time employment. Some firms, such as Robert Half International (www.rhii. com) specialize in certain types of workers, such as accounting, law, information technology, and computer personnel.

If you are interested in "testing the job waters," you may want to contact these firms for information on their services. Employers – not job seekers – pay for these services. While many of these firms are listed in your community Yellow Pages, most have websites. The following websites are especially popular with individuals interested in part-time, temporary, or contract work: www.net-temps.com, www.elance.com, www.ework. com, www.guru.com, and www.talentmarket.monster. com.

4. **College/university placement offices**

College and university placement offices provide in-house career planning services for graduating students. While some give assistance to alumni, don't expect too much help if you have already graduated; you may, instead, need to contact the alumni office which may offer employment services. Many college placement offices are understaffed or provide only rudimentary services, such as maintaining a career planning library, coordinating on-campus interviews for graduating seniors, and conducting workshops on how to write resumes and interview. Others provide a full range of well supported services including testing and one-on-one counseling. Indeed, many community colleges offer such services to members of the community on a walk-in basis. You can use their libraries and computerized career assessment programs, take personality and interest inventories, or attend special workshops or full-semester career planning courses which will take you through each step of the career planning and job search processes. You may want to enroll in such a course since it is likely to provide just enough structure and content to assess your motivated abilities and skills and to assist you in implementing a successful job search plan. Check with your local campus to see what services you might use.

Many of the college and university placement offices belong to the National Association of Colleges and Employers, which operates its own employment website: www.jobweb.com. This site includes a wealth of information on employment for college graduates (see the "Site Map" section: www.jobweb.com/search/sitemap.htm). Its "Career Library" section includes direct links to hundreds of college and university placement offices: www.jobweb.com/Career_Development/college res.htm. To find college alumni offices, visit the following websites: www.alumni.net, www.bcharrispub.com, and www.jobweb.com/After_College. Since colleges and universities tend to be very web-savvy, you can visit hundreds of their career websites to acquire all types of useful free information on conducting an effective job search. One of my favorites is the website operated by the Career Center at the College of William and Mary (www.wm.edu/career). Indeed, searching many of these college and university websites is comparable to having your own personal career counselor – without having to go to college!

5.   Private career and job search firms

Private career and job search firms help individuals acquire job search skills and coach them through the process of finding a job. They do not find you a job. In other words, they teach you much of what is outlined in this book. Expect to pay anywhere from $1,500 to $10,000 for this service. If you need a structured environment for conducting your job search, contract with one of these firms for professional assistance. One of the major such firms used to be Bernard Haldane Associates (they ceased operating in 2004). Many of their pioneering career planning and job search methods are incorporated in this book as well as can be found in five other key job search books: _Haldane's Best Resumes for Professionals, Haldane's Best Cover Letters for Professionals, Haldane's Best Answers to Tough Interview Questions, Haldane's Best Salary Tips for Professionals_, and _Haldane's Best Employment Websites for Professionals_ (Impact Publications – see the order form at the end of this book or www.impactpublications.com). Other firms offering similar services include Right Management Associates (www.right.com), R. L. Stevens & Associates (www.interviewing.com), and Lee Hecht Harrison (www.lhh.com/us).

6. Executive search firms and headhunters

Executive search firms work for employers seeking employees to fill critical positions in the $50,000 plus salary range. They also are called "headhunters," "management consultants,"and "executive recruiters." These firms play an important role in linking high level technical and managerial talent to organizations. Don't expect to contract for these services. Executive recruiters work for employers, not applicants. If a friend or relative is in this business or you have relevant skills of interest to these firms, let them know you are available – and ask for their advice. On the other hand, you may want to contact firms that specialize in recruiting individuals with your skill specialty.

For a comprehensive listing of these firms, see the latest edition of _The Directory of Executive Recruiters_ (Kennedy Information, www.kennedyinfo.com; also see the order form at the end of this book or www.impactpublications.com). Several companies, such as www.resumezapper.com, www.blastmyresume.com, and www.resumeblaster.com, offer email resume blasting services that primarily target headhunters. For a fee, which usually ranges from $50 to $200, these firms will blast your resume to 5,000 to 10,000 headhunters. This is a quick, easy, and inexpensive way to reach thousands of headhunters and executive search firms. This resume distribution method also may be a waste of time and money. Approach it with a sense of healthy skepticism.

7. Marketing services

Marketing services represent an interesting combination of job search and executive search activities. They can cost $2,500 or more, and they work with individuals anticipating a starting salary of at least $75,000 but preferably over $100,000. These firms try to minimize the time and risk of applying for jobs. A typical operation begins with a client paying a $150 fee for developing psychological, skills, and interests profiles. If you pass this stage – most anyone with money does – you go on to the next one-on-one stage. At this point, a marketing plan is outlined and a contract signed for specific services. Work for the client usually involves activities centered on the resume and interviewing. Using word processing software, the firm normally develops a slick "professional" resume and sends it by mail or e-mail, along with a cover letter, to hundreds – maybe thousands – of firms. Clients are then briefed and sent to interview with interested employers. While you can save money and achieve the same results on your own, these firms do have one major advantage: They save you **time** by doing most of the work for you. Again, approach these services with caution and with the knowledge that you can probably do just as well – if not better – on your own by following the step-by-step advice of this and other job search books.

8. Women's centers and special career services

Women's centers and special career services for displaced workers, such as 40-Plus Clubs (see www.fortyplus.org for a directory of these clubs in 12 states plus the District of Columbia) and Five O'Clock Clubs (www.fiveoclockclub.com), have been established to respond to the employment needs of special groups. Women's centers are particularly active in sponsoring career planning workshops and job information networks. These centers tend to be geared toward elementary job search activities, because many of their clientele consist of homemakers who are entering or re-entering the workforce with little knowledge of the job market. Special career services arise at times for different categories of employees. For example, unemployed aerospace engineers, teachers, veterans, air traffic controllers, and government employees have formed special groups for developing job search skills and sharing job leads.

9. Testing and assessment centers

Testing and assessment centers provide assistance for identifying vocational skills, interests, and objectives. Usually staffed by trained professionals, these centers administer several types of tests and charge from $200 to $900 per person. If you use such services, make sure you are given one or both of the two most popular and reliable tests: *Myers-Briggs Type Indicator®* and the *Strong Interest Inventory®*. You should find both tests helpful in better understanding your interests and decision-making styles. In many cases, the career office at your local community college or women's center can administer these tests at minimum cost ($20 to $40). At the same time, many of these testing and assessment services are now available online. Check out these popular websites: www.skillsone.com, www.self-directed-search.com, www.careerlab.com, www.personalityonline.com, www.assessment.com, and www.personalitytype.com.

10. Job fairs and career conferences

Job fairs and career conferences are organized by a variety of groups – from schools and government agencies to headhunters, employment agencies, and professional associations – to link applicants to employers. **Job fairs** are often open to the public and involve many employers. **Career conferences** may be closed to the public (invitation only) and involve a single employer. Usually consisting of one- to two-day meetings in a hotel or conference center, employers meet with applicants as a group and on a one-to-one basis. Employers give presentations on their companies, applicants circulate resumes, and employers interview candidates. Many such conferences are organized to attract hard-to-recruit groups, such as engineers, computer programmers, individuals with security clearances, and clerical and service workers, or for special population groups, such as minorities, transitioning military personnel, women, people with disabilities, and even ex-offenders. These are excellent sources for job leads and information on specific employers and jobs – if you are invited to attend or if the meeting is open to the public. Employers pay for this service, although some job fairs and career conferences may charge job seekers a nominal registration fee.

11. Professional associations

Professional associations often provide placement assistance. This usually consists of listing job vacancies in publications, maintaining a resume database, and organizing a job information exchange at annual conferences. Some may even organize job fairs, such as the Military Officers Association of America (www.moaa.org) and the NonCommissioned Officers Association (www.ncoausa.org). Many large associations operate their own online employment sites; members can include their resume in an electronic database and employers can access the database to search for qualified candidates. Annual conferences are good sources for making job contacts in different geographic locations within a particular professional field. But don't expect too much. Talking to people (networking) at professional conferences may yield better results than reading job listings, placing your resume in a database, or interviewing at conference placement centers. For excellent online directories of professional associations, be sure to visit these two sites: www.ipl.org/ref/aon and www.asaenet.org.

12. Professional resume writers

Professional resume writers are increasingly playing an important role in career planning. Each year thousands of job seekers rely on these professionals for assistance in writing their resumes. Many of these professionals also provide useful job search tips on resume distribution, cover letters, and networking as well as include other career planning and job search services, such as assessment, mentoring, coaching, and practice interviewing. Charging from $100 to $600 for writing a resume, they work with the whole spectrum of job seekers – entry-level to senior executives making millions of dollars each year. While some are certified career counselors, many of these professionals have their own associations and certification groups that include a large assortment of often unintelligible initials after their names – CAC, CBC, CCM, CEIP, CHRE, CIPC, CPC, CPRW, JCTC, LPC, NBCC, NCC, NCCC, NCRW, and PCC. If you are interested in working with a professional resume writer, visit the following websites for information on this network of career professionals: www.parw.com, www.prwra.com, www.cmi.com, and www.nrwaweb.com. Examples of their high-end work can be found in my three resume books – *High Impact Resumes and Letters, Blue-Collar Resume and Job Hunting Guide*, and *Military-to-Civilian Transition Resumes and Letters* – and in most of Wendy Enelow's books, such as *Best Resumes for $100,000+ Jobs* and *Best Cover Letters for $100,000+ Jobs* (Impact Publications – see order form at the end of this book or visit them online: www.impactpublications.com).

13. Certified Career Professionals

Certified career professionals are experienced in working one-on-one with clients, with special emphasis on career assessment. They have their own professional associations. If you are interested in contacting a certified career professional for assistance, we advise you to first visit these websites:

- **National Board for Certified Counselors, Inc.**   www.nbcc.org
- **National Career Development Association**   www.ncda.org
- **Certified Career Coaches**   www.certifiedcareer coaches.com

- **Career Planning and Adult
  Development Network**   www.careernetwork.org

You also can find a great deal of professional career assistance through the U.S. Department of Labor's website, which enables users to locate services within their communities:

- **America's Service Locator**   www.servicelocator.org

Whatever you do, be a smart shopper for career planning and job search services. Proceed with caution, know exactly what you are getting into, and choose the best. Remember, there is no such thing as a free lunch, and you often get less than what you pay for. At the same time, the most expensive services are not necessarily the best. Indeed, the free and inexpensive career planning services offered by many community or junior colleges – libraries, computerized career assessment programs, testing, and workshops – may be all you need. On the other hand, don't be afraid to spend some money on getting the best services for your needs. You may quickly discover that this money was well spent when you land a job that pays 20 to 40 percent more than your previous job! Whatever you do, don't be *"pennywise but pound foolish"* by trying to do your job search on the cheap. If you have difficulty writing a first-class resume, by all means contact a resume-writing pro who can put together a dynamite resume that truly represents what you have done, can do, and will do in the future.

> *The free and inexpensive career planning services offered by many community colleges – libraries, testing, and workshops – may be all you need.*

After reading this book, you should be able to make intelligent decisions about what, when, where, and with what results you can use professional assistance. Shop around, compare services and costs, ask questions, talk to former clients, and read the fine print before giving an employment expert a job using your hard earned money. Don't try to be the Lone Ranger all of the time. If necessary, contact a career professional at different stages of your job search. A career expert could very well become your best friend for deciding exactly what you want to do in the future!

TIP #14
Conduct your job search while being employed.

It's best to conduct your job search while you have a job. Even though you can spend more time looking for a job if you are not working, you may have difficulty explaining your unemployment to prospective employers, who prefer hiring people who are currently employed. Unemployed people simply have less value than employed people. If you are out of work, you will be in a weak negotiation position when it comes time to deal with salary and benefit issues. In addition, being employed will help you with the financial costs of conducting a job search. If you have been laid off or fired, consider temporary employment or make your job search an 80-hour a week endeavor. Whatever you do, you need to be very busy working toward your new employment future. A job search can easily become a full-time job!

TIP #15
Check the quality of your writing, interpersonal communication, and public speaking skills.

Employers want to work with individuals who are good and effective communicators. Indeed, communication skills – writing, interpersonal, and public speaking – rank very high on employers' lists of the most desirable skills in employees, often ahead of specific technical skills. If your communication skills need improvement, by all means seek help. Contact an adult education program through your local school district or a community or junior college for assistance. You'll find various courses, from basic reading, spelling, vocabulary, grammar, and listening, to computer, business writing, and public speaking, available through such programs and colleges. These skills are key to finding good jobs, getting ahead on the job, and advancing careers. They will follow you throughout your worklife. In fact, giving a speech is ranked as the number one fear – outranking death, which is number six! Most important of all, each year thousands of individuals pass up promotions because of the fear of giving briefings, speeches, and presentations that normally go with many promotions. If you are a reluctant communicator, consider joining one of the many Toastmasters groups for developing presentation skills in a non-threatening, supportive environment (www.toastmasters.org or 1-800-993-7732) as well as acquire a copy of Caryl Krannich's *101 Secrets of Highly Effective Speakers* (Impact Publications). See the order form at the end of this book.

TIP #16
Keep enthusiastic and motivated throughout your job search.

Let's face it. Few people can maintain the same level of energy, enthusiasm, and motivation throughout a three- to six-month job search. It's especially difficult when they encounter numerous rejections along the way. Indeed, the number one problem most job seekers encounter and have difficulty dealing with is rejections. Accustomed to being successful in other aspects of their lives, they find a job search can be very ego deflating. In fact, most people can handle three rejections in a row, but four, five, six, or seven rejections are difficult to deal with.

> *The number one problem most job seekers encounter and have difficulty dealing with is rejections.*

Faced with a string of rejections, many job seekers become demoralized, cut back on their job search activities, or just go through the motions of looking for a job by sending out more resumes and letters in response to classified ads and online job postings. But there are certain things you can do to keep yourself focused and motivated. First, treat rejections as part of the game. You can't get acceptances before acquiring numerous rejections. Consider the typical job search which goes something like this:

No, No, No, No, No, No, Maybe, No, No, No, Yes, No, No, No
No, No, No, Maybe, No, Maybe, Yes, No, No, No, No, Yes, Yes

If you get disillusioned and quit after receiving four rejections, you will prematurely fail. You need to continue "collecting" more rejections in order to get an acceptance. In fact, we often recommend that individuals get up in the morning with the idea of collecting at least 20 rejections! You will eventually get acceptances, but you must first deal with many rejections on the road to success. How you deal with rejections may largely determine how successful you will be in your job search, career, and life. If you identify what it is you want to do but cannot implement the necessary changes because you fear rejection, you will be going nowhere with your future.

Second, reward yourself after achieving certain goals. For example, let's say your goal this week is to send out 20 resumes, make 35 networking calls, and arrange four informational interviews. If you start on Monday and achieve these goals by Thursday, reward yourself by taking Friday off or go out for dinner at your favorite restaurant. Try to build a system of rewards related to specific goals so that you can occasionally celebrate successes. These little rewards will help keep you focused and motivated throughout your job search. Remember, this is a slow and unpredictable process that takes time and requires a positive approach to rejections.

Third, if you become depressed and find it difficult to get motivated and active, take a few days off and engage in some useful volunteer work to recharge your batteries. Helping other people deal with their problems – be it housing, hunger, employment, or illness – will give you a different perspective on life. Chances are it will provide a fresh perspective on your situation and help motivate you to get back on track with your job search. Indeed, changing your environment by associating with different people and situations can be refreshing.

TIP #17
Try to mend any broken fences with previous employers.

If you left a previous employer on less than good terms – you were fired or resigned in anger – and you know that employer may be contacted by a prospective employer, do whatever you can to mend fences. Consider calling the previous employer and explain what you have been doing since you left him or her. If you've turned a new chapter in your life, share your changes with the individual. If you need to apologize for any past behavior, this would be a good time to do so. Mention that you are in the process of looking for a job, and explain the nature of the job and your related skills. Most important of all, ask if this individual would be willing to give you a positive recommendation. Your goal here should be to at least neutralize what could become a negative recommendation if left on its own. It's always best to neutralize a relationship rather than let it fester and become negative. In many cases, time is a great healer of difficult relationships. You first need to get over any negative feelings you may have toward your previous employer. Chances are your previous employer has probably gotten over you; he or she will probably wish you well and not say anything negative about you to your future employer. In some cases, the individual may become one of your strongest supporters and may even recommend you to other employers. Always remember the importance of relationships in your job search, on the job, and in your life. Individuals with lots of friends, supportive relationships, and active networks are in a good position to make job and career changes with relative ease. Be sure to constantly develop, nurture, and expand your network of relationships. People with not-so-hot backgrounds will need to pay particular attention to mending and nurturing relationships that could work against their best interests.

TIP #18
Pick your references carefully, make them aware of your job search, and ask for their assistance.

Employers are suspicious of strangers, which means most job seekers. Many are rightfully suspicious because they have previously encountered problems with candidates who have misrepresented their qualifications. In fact, research has found that nearly 70 percent of job seekers lie on their resumes. As a result of bad hiring decisions, employers increasingly conduct background checks and follow through on references provided by candidates. A thorough background check may uncover everything from your employment history and housing situation to credit history and any criminal activity. If, for example, you have been convicted of a crime, chances are that conviction will be revealed during a routine background check. As many ex-offenders quickly discover, there are few places to hide these days given the use of computerized databases and background checks.

In addition to contacting previous employers, many employers will ask for a list of references and then check them accordingly. While many previous employers will only verify employment and attendance records, many employers and references will respond to this often asked and revealing question posed by reference checkers:

> *"Knowing what you do about this individual, would you hire him again today?"*

A definite "Yes" is a strong recommendation. A "No," "Maybe," or "Not Sure" could raise red flags in the mind of a prospective employer. Therefore, it's very important that you choose your references wisely and contact them as well as previous employers (those who employed you during the past 10 years only) about your impending job change. Send these individuals a copy of your resume along with an explanation of your current employment situation, interests, and skills. Not only is this a

> *Employers are rightfully suspicious of candidates since nearly 70 percent lie on their resumes. As a result, employers increasingly conduct background checks and contact references.*

wise thing to do, it's also a very professional and thoughtful action on your part. You don't want a prospective employer contacting a previous employer or reference and receive this response:

> *"Oh, I didn't know he was looking for a job again. What's he up to these days?"*

Instead, you want the individual to speak authoritatively about you, your accomplishments and character, and how you might be perfect for this job:

"Yes, I would delighted to tell you about him. This job sounds like a perfect fit for both you and Tom."

Many individuals you contact as references also may play important roles in your network. Consider this an important networking activity that may result in useful advice and referrals.

TIP #19
Join or organize a job search club or support group.

You can significantly improve the effectiveness of your job search, as well as shorten your job search time, by involving others in your job search. Involve your family, friends, and others who are interested in conducting a job search. If you're married, your spouse should become a member of your support group.

Job clubs are designed to provide a group structure and support system to individuals seeking employment. These groups consist of about 12 individuals who are led by a trained counselor and supported with computers, telephones, copying machines, and a resource center. Formal job clubs, such as the 40-Plus Clubs (www.fortyplus.org) and the Five O'Clock Clubs (www.fiveoclockclub.com), organize job search activities for both the advertised and hidden job markets. Job club activities may include:

- Signing commitment agreements to achieve specific job search goals and targets.

- Contacting friends, relatives, and acquaintances for job leads.

- Completing activity forms.

- Using telephones, computers, photocopy machines, postage, and other equipment and supplies.

- Meeting with fellow participants to discuss job search progress.

- Meeting with career counselors or other career specialists.

- Attending job fairs and hiring conferences.

- Telephoning to uncover job leads.

- Using the Internet to research the job market and contact potential employers.

- Researching newspapers, telephone books, and directories.

- Developing research, telephone, interview, and social skills.

- Writing letters and resumes.

- Responding to employment ads.

- Completing employment applications.

- Assessing weekly progress and sharing information with fellow group members.

In other words, the job club formalizes many of the prospecting, networking, and informational interviewing activities within a group context and interjects the role of the telephone as the key communication device for developing and expanding networks.

Many job clubs place excessive reliance on using the telephone and Internet for uncovering job leads. Members cold-call prospective employers and ask about job openings. The Yellow Pages and the Internet become the job hunter's best friends. During a two-week period, a job club member might spend most of his or her mornings telephoning for job leads and scheduling interviews. Afternoons are normally devoted to job interviewing.

Many job club methods are designed for individuals who need a job – any job – quickly. Since individuals try to fit into available vacancies, their specific objectives and skills are of secondary concern. Other job club methods are more consistent with the focus and methods outlined in this book, especially those used by 40-Plus Clubs and Five O'Clock Clubs.

In lieu of participating in such clubs, you may want to form your own **support group** that adapts some job club methods around our central concept of finding a job fit for you – one appropriate to your objective and in line with your particular mix of skills, abilities, and interests. Support groups are a useful alternative to job clubs. They have one major advantage to conducting a job search on your own: they may cut your job search time in half because they provide an important structure for achieving goals. Forming or joining one of these groups can help direct as well as enhance your individual job search activities.

Your support group should consist of three or more individuals who are job hunting. Try to schedule regular meetings with specific purposes in mind. While the group may be highly social, especially if working with close friends, it also should be **task-oriented**. Meet at least once a week and include your spouse. At each meeting set **performance goals** for the week. For example, your goal can be to make 20 new contacts and conduct five informational interviews. The contacts can be made by telephone, email, letter, or in person. Share your experiences and job information with each other. **Critique** each other's progress, make suggestions for improving the job search, and develop new strategies together. By doing this, you will be gaining valuable information and feedback which is normally difficult to gain on your own. This group should provide important psychological supports to help you through your job search. After all, job hunting can be a lonely, frustrating, and exasperating experience. By sharing your experiences with others, you will find you are not alone. You will quickly learn that rejections are part of the game. The group will encourage you, and you will feel good about helping others achieve their goals. Try building small incentives into the group, such as the individual who receives the most job interviews for the month will be treated to dinner by other members of the group.

> *Job hunting can be a lonely, frustrating, and exasperating experience. Sharing your experiences with a support group can provide important psychological supports to help you through your job search.*

TIP #20
Try to find a job that's fit for you rather than one you feel you can fit into.

Most individuals look for jobs they think they might be able to do. Many of them see jobs that look interesting and then try to stretch their qualifications on their resume in order to fit into the job. Unfortunately, many individuals end up in jobs that really don't fit them. They end up bored with their work, use skills they really don't like using, and have difficulty keeping focused and motivated. Had these individuals approached their job search by first assessing their motivated abilities and skills and developed an objective for organizing their job search around their strengths, they would have looked for jobs that were fit for them rather than ones they might fit into. Whatever you do, make sure you look for jobs that are fit for you.

TIP #21
Use a temporary employment agency for quickly finding employment and acquiring experience and contacts.

If you're not sure what you want to do, or if you lost your job and need to quickly find employment and receive a paycheck, consider contacting a temporary employment firm. Most communities have several such companies that specialize in providing employees for different occupations. Many large temporary firms, such as Manpower, Kelly Services, Olsten, Labor Finders, and Robert Half International, operate nationally. These companies regularly place individuals in part-time and full-time hourly positions at all levels. While assignments may be for as little as one day with an employer, other assignments may be for several weeks. Many of these firms also have temp-to-perm programs for individuals interested in permanent employment. These programs place individuals in positions for two- to three-month periods after which an employer decides whether to hire the individual. These services and programs can be excellent for individuals who need to gain work experience, meet different employers, and have a regular pay check. Best of all, these services give job seekers flexibility when looking for a job since they can choose their hours and are not committed to any single employer.

TIP #22
Always ask questions, but avoid becoming an interrogator during a job interview.

Conducting an effective job search requires asking lots of questions of many individuals. You need to be intellectually curious about jobs, employers, organizations, skills, opportunities, and other important aspects of finding and keeping a job if you are to make intelligent decisions concerning your future. After all, not only do you want to impress upon employers that you are the right person for the job, which you do when you ask questions, you also need information to determine if you want to work for particular employers. Much of your job search should involve research – gathering information from others about different jobs, employers, companies, communities, and salaries and benefits. Above all, learn who has the power to hire, how you can best approach a company for a job, and what it is like working for particular organizations and individuals. You'll especially want to ask questions during job interviews. Develop a list of questions you should ask of employers and the identify three or four questions you want to ask near the end of the interview. Keep your questions to a minimum so you don't intimidate the interviewer with a litany of questions that make you appear to be an interrogator. For a good introduction to the type of questions you should ask at a job interview, see Richard Fein's *101 Dynamite Questions to Ask At Your Job Interview* (Impact Publications). See the order form at the end of this book.

TIP #23
Be a good listener.

Listening is an active skill that can be learned. Being a good listener takes effort. It requires active involvement. One of the major errors job seekers make is talking too much and listening too little. Especially during job interviews, employers are turned off by candidates who constantly talk but seem not to be interested in listening to what the interviewer or others are saying. Since most people interpret no response as a negative response, avoid an expressionless face when listening to others. Try to become a good listener by acquiring several nonverbal behaviors associated with active listening:

- Focus on what is being said rather than thinking about how the other person looks, what you want to say next, or your nervousness or fear of not getting a job offer.

- Listen objectively for content and avoid being distracted by any annoying words, ideas, or mannerisms of others.

- Try to listen for information and withhold evaluation of the message until later.

- Give positive feedback by occasionally nodding in agreement and smiling – indications of interest on your part in the speaker and what is being said.

> *Minimize rejections by developing an active networking campaign involving informational interviews. If approached properly, over 50 percent of individuals you ask for an informational interview will agree to speak with you.*

If you try to concentrate on what is being said rather than on how you are doing, you will probably make a good impression on other people. Being other-directed with your nonverbal communication will make you seem more likable and competent than candidates who are noticeably self-concerned and nervous throughout the interview.

TIP #24
Prepare to handle rejections with a positive attitude and plan of action.

As we noted in Tip #16, rejections are a big part of any job search. Everyone encounters them – not just people with red flags in their backgrounds. How you handle rejections may determine how success-ful you are in finding the right job for you. If you become discouraged because of rejections, you'll have difficulty keeping motivated, main-taining a positive attitude, and taking appropriate actions for advanc-ing your job search. But if you know you need to experience many rejections before encountering a single acceptance, you should be able to develop a plan of action that keeps you focused on achieving your goals. One of the best ways to handle rejections and stay motivated is to join a job search club or form your own support group, as we outlined in Tip #19. Working with others will help you maintain a positive attitude and focus on getting a few important acceptances – invitations to job interviews – as you navigate through a sea of rejections.

One of the most important ways to minimize rejections is to develop an active networking campaign involving informational interviews – interviews you conduct to gather information, advice, and referrals. If approached properly, over 50 percent of individuals you ask for an informational interview will agree to speak and/or meet with you. That's a much higher acceptance rate than you will get from sending resumes or completing applications in response to job vacan-cies. Many informational interviews also lead to actual job interviews and offers. For information on how to minimize rejections through networking and informational interviews, see my two networking and interviewing books, *The Savvy Networker* and *You Should Hire Me!* (Impact Publications). See order form at the end of this book.

TIP #25
Don't buy into the snake oil approaches of motivational gurus and positive thinkers for conducting a job search.

Your best approach to finding a job is to focus on your motivated abilities and skills (see Chapter 3), which constitute your major strengths – those things you do well and enjoy doing. While it's important to have dreams, set goals, follow your passions, and be a positive thinker, it's also important to be realistic about what you can and will do for employers. Know who you really are before venturing out into the job market. Unfortunately, many job seekers have unrealistic expectations of what jobs they can do. Some get pumped up on positive thinking, which may motivate them to get through the day, but positive thinking without the necessary qualifications can lead to psychological crashes and depression. The positive thinking preachings of motivational gurus help many people in sales positions get through their days, which are filled with the numerous rejections attendant with making cold calls as part of a routine prospecting campaign. Not surprisingly, these salespeople disproportionately attend motivational seminars, listen to motivational tapes, and read motivational books. But this approach has limited usefulness for those conducting a job search. Employers look for substance – not just for individuals pumped up on positive thinking and high self-esteem. Be positive, energetic, and enthusiastic, but try being your best by presenting your best self to employers. For a good examination of how to best approach your job search devoid of such snake oil, see Barbara Sher's *I Can Do Anything If I Only Knew What It Was* (Dell), *It's Only Too Late If You Don't Start Now* (Dell), *Live the Life You Love* (Dell), and *Wishcraft: How to Get What You Really Want* (Random House). See the order form at the end of this book.

TIP #26
Put together a list of red flags that could become potential job knockouts.

We all have red flags in our backgrounds. What are yours? Perhaps you dropped out of school, failed an important test, lost a job, experienced financial difficulties, got divorced, became seriously ill, lack experience and goals, have a criminal record, abused drugs or alcohol, don't relate well to others, appear over-qualified, have work-related problems and poor references, have a learning disorder or physical handicap, or are a job hopper with an unstable work history. Most red flags relate to health, legal, financial, personal, learning, and behavioral problems in your past. For employers, such red flags reveal potential on-the-job problems they would like to avoid. If you have any red flags in your background that are likely to become employment issues, you need to deal with these **before** they become potential knock-outs on resumes, in job interviews, or on the job.

If you have ever been fired for the following high-risk behaviors, you have red flags in your background which may knock you out of consideration for a job should the employer learn about them from your references or a background check:

- Absent and tardy
- Broke rules
- Insubordinate
- Lying
- Stealing
- Uncooperative
- Drug and alcohol abuse
- Fighting on the job
- Bad attitude
- Dishonest
- Incompetent
- Abuse coworkers or clients
- Unpredictable behavior
- Lazy and undependable

Respond to the following statements to determine how "not-so-hot" your background may be. Circle the numbers to the right of each statement that best represents your degree of agreement or disagreement:

1 = Strongly agree	4 = Disagree
2 = Agree	5 = Strongly disagree
3 = Uncertain	

		1	2	3	4	5
1.	I have little work experience.	1	2	3	4	5
2.	I have work experience, but it is doing very different work from what I want to do.	1	2	3	4	5
3.	My grades in school were not very good.	1	2	3	4	5
4.	I lack a high school diploma or GED.	1	2	3	4	5
5.	I did not go to college or I dropped out of college.	1	2	3	4	5
6.	I have been fired from one job.	1	2	3	4	5
7.	I have been fired from more than one job.	1	2	3	4	5
8.	I have held several jobs in the last three years.	1	2	3	4	5
9.	The jobs I have held have each been very different from each other in terms of the work to be done and skills required.	1	2	3	4	5

10. I don't have a past employer who
    would give me a good reference.   1   2   3   4   5

11. I have been convicted of a felony.   1   2   3   4   5

12. I have a learning disability.   1   2   3   4   5

13. I have difficulty relating to others.   1   2   3   4   5

14. I've experienced some major health
    problems.   1   2   3   4   5

15. I've experienced marital problems.   1   2   3   4   5

16. My financial situation is difficult.   1   2   3   4   5

17. I've abused drugs and/or alcohol.   1   2   3   4   5

18. I have an arrest record.   1   2   3   4   5

19. If an employer knew much about my
    employment background, I would
    probably not be hired.   1   2   3   4   5

20. If an employer knew much about my
    background, I probably would not be hired. 1   2   3   4   5

21. I appear over-qualified.   1   2   3   4   5

TOTAL

If you circled a "1" or "2" for any of these statements, you may raise a red flag in the eyes of most employers. If your total score is between 26 and 60, you will most likely appear to have a not-so-hot background in the eyes of most employers. You'll need to develop job search strategies to overcome your job market weaknesses.

The first thing you need to do in dealing with red flags is to identify and acknowledge them as potential job knock-outs. Denying them or making excuses will not help you take corrective actions that can make you more employable. Once you've identified your red flags, the next step is to develop strategies for turning red flags into green flags that tell employers that you will be a good hire. You can start this process by asking yourself the following questions:

1. What questions might an employer ask concerning my background that could raise red flags about my fitness for the job?

2 What five things about my background could knock me out of consideration for a job?

3. What past red flag behaviors might I need to re-examine and take greater responsibility for in the future?

4. What positive actions have I taken to change the negative behaviors that raise red flags?

5. Why would someone want to hire me?

6. What are my best work characteristics?

For more information on potential red flags affecting a job search and how to best deal with them, see my book, *Job Interview Tips for People With Not-So-Hot Backgrounds* (Impact Publications). See the order form at the end of this book.

TIP #27
Test your ability to conduct a
well-organized job search.

Just how prepared are you to organize and implement an effective job search? Let's answer this question by testing your current level of job search information, skills, and strategies as well as identifying those you need to develop and improve. Identify your level of job search competence by completing the following exercise:

INSTRUCTIONS: Respond to each statement by circling which number at the right best represents your situation.

SCALE: 1 = Strongly agree   4 = Disagree
            2 = Agree   5 = Strongly disagree
            3 = Maybe, not certain

1. I know what motivates me to excel at work.   1   2   3   4   5

2. I can identify my strongest abilities and skills.   1   2   3   4   5

3. I have seven major achievements that clarify a pattern of interests and abilities that are relevant to my job and career.   1   2   3   4   5

4. I know what I both like and dislike in work.   1   2   3   4   5

5. I know what I want to do during the next 10 years.   1   2   3   4   5

6. I have a well defined career objective that focuses my job search on particular organizations and employers.   1   2   3   4   5

7. I know what skills I can offer employers in different occupations.   1   2   3   4   5

8. I know what skills employers most seek in candidates.   1   2   3   4   5

9. I can clearly explain to employers what I do well and enjoy doing.   1   2   3   4   5

10. I can specify why employers should hire me.   1   2   3   4   5

11. I can gain the support of family and friends for making a job or career change.   1   2   3   4   5

12. I can find 10 to 20 hours a week to conduct a part-time job search.   1   2   3   4   5

13. I have the financial ability to sustain a three-month job search.   1   2   3   4   5

14. I can conduct library and Internet research on different occupations, employers, organizations, and communities.   1   2   3   4   5

15. I can write different types of effective resumes and job search/thank you letters.   1   2   3   4   5

16. I can produce and distribute resumes and letters to the right people.   1   2   3   4   5

17. I can list my major accomplishments in
     action terms.   1   2   3   4   5

18. I can identify and target employers I want
     to interview.   1   2   3   4   5

19. I know how to use the Internet to conduct
     employment research and network.   1   2   3   4   5

20. I know which websites are best for posting
     my resumes and browsing job postings.   1   2   3   4   5

21. I know how much time I should spend
     conducting an online job search.   1   2   3   4   5

22. I can develop a job referral network.   1   2   3   4   5

23. I can persuade others to join in forming
     a job search support group.   1   2   3   4   5

24. I can prospect for job leads.   1   2   3   4   5

25. I can use the telephone to develop prospects
     and get referrals and interviews.   1   2   3   4   5

26. I can plan and implement an effective
     direct-mail job search campaign.   1   2   3   4   5

27. I can persuade employers to interview me.   1   2   3   4   5

28. I have a list of at least 10 employer-centered
     questions I need to ask during interviews.   1   2   3   4   5

29. I know the best time to talk about salary
     with an employer.   1   2   3   4   5

30. I know what I want to do with my life over
     the next 10 years.   1   2   3   4   5

31. I have a clear pattern of accomplishments
     which I can explain to employers with
     examples.   1   2   3   4   5

32. I have little difficulty in making cold calls
     and striking up conversations with strangers.   1   2   3   4   5

33. I usually take responsibility for my own
actions rather than blame other people for
my situation or circumstance. 1 2 3 4 5

34. I can generate at least one job interview
for every 10 job search contacts I make. 1 2 3 4 5

35. I can follow up on job interviews. 1 2 3 4 5

36. I can negotiate a salary 10-20% above
what an employer initially offers. 1 2 3 4 5

37. I can persuade an employer to renegotiate
my salary after six months on the job. 1 2 3 4 5

38. I can create a position for myself in
an organization. 1 2 3 4 5

TOTAL [   ]

Calculate your overall potential job search effectiveness by adding the numbers you circled for a composite score. If your total is more than 90 points, you need to work on developing your job search. How you scored each item will indicate to what degree you need to work on improving specific job search skills. If your score is under 60 points, you are well on your way toward job search success!

TIP #28
Follow 20 key principles to
job search success.

Success is determined by more than just a good plan getting implemented. We know success is not determined primarily by intelligence, time management, positive thinking, or luck. Based upon experience, theory, research, common sense, and acceptance of some self-transformation principles, we believe you will achieve job search success by following most of these 20 principles:

1. **You should work hard at finding a job:** Make this a daily endeavor and involve your family. Focus on specifics.

2. **You should not be discouraged by setbacks:** You are playing the odds, so expect disappointments and handle them in stride. You will get many "no's" before finding the one "yes" which is right for you.

3. **You should be patient and persevere:** Expect three to six months of hard work before you connect with the job that's right for you.

4. **You should be honest with yourself and others:** Honesty is always the best policy. But don't be naive and stupid by confessing your negatives and shortcomings to others.

5. **You should develop a positive attitude toward yourself:** Nobody wants to employ guilt-ridden people with inferiority complexes. Focus on your positive characteristics.

6. **You should associate with very positive and successful people:** Finding a job largely depends on how well you relate to others. Avoid associating with negative and depressing people who complain and have a "you-can't-do-it" attitude. Run with winners who have a positive "can-do" outlook on life.

7. **You should set goals:** You should have a clear idea of what you want and where you are going. Without these, you will present a confusing and indecisive image to others. Clear goals direct your job search into productive channels. Setting high goals will help make you work hard in getting what you want.

8. **You should plan:** Convert your goals into action steps that are organized as short, intermediate, and long-range plans.

9. **You should get organized:** Translate your plans into activities, targets, names, addresses, telephone numbers, and materials. Develop an efficient and effective filing system and use a large calendar to set time targets, record appointments, and compile useful information.

10. **You should be a good communicator:** Take stock of your oral, written, and nonverbal communication skills. How well do you communicate? Since most aspects of your job search involve communicating with others, and communication skills are one of the most sought-after skills, always present yourself well both verbally and nonverbally.

11. **You should be energetic and enthusiastic:** Employers are attracted to positive people. They don't like negative and depressing people who toil at their work. Generate enthusiasm both verbally and nonverbally. Check on your telephone voice with a friend or relative – it may be more unenthusiastic than your face-to-face voice.

12. **You should ask questions:** Your best information comes from asking questions. Learn to develop intelligent questions that are non-aggressive, polite, and interesting to others. But don't ask too many questions and thereby become a bore.

13. **You should be a good listener:** Being a good listener is often more important than being a good questioner or talker. Learn to improve your face-to-face listening behavior (nonverbal cues) as well as remember and use information gained from others. Make others feel they enjoyed talking with you, i.e., you are one of the few people who actually **listens** to what they say.

14. **You should be civil, which means being polite, courteous, and thoughtful:** Treat gatekeepers, especially receptionists, like human beings. Avoid being aggressive. Try to be polite, courteous, and gracious. Your social graces are being observed. Remember to send thank you letters – a very thoughtful thing to do in a job search. Even if rejected, thank employers for the "opportunity." They may later have additional opportunities, and they will remember you.

15. **You should be tactful:** Watch what you say to others about people. Don't be a gossip, back-stabber, or confessor.

16. **You should maintain a professional stance:** Be neat in what you do and wear, and speak with the confidence, authority, and maturity of a professional.

17. **You should demonstrate your intelligence and competence:** Present yourself as someone who gets things done and achieves results – a **producer**. Employers generally seek people who are bright, hard working, responsible, communicate well, have positive personalities, maintain good interpersonal relations, are likable, observe dress and social codes, take initiative, are talented, possess expertise in particular areas, use good judgment, are cooperative, trustworthy, and loyal, generate confidence and credibility, and are conventional. In other words, they like people who score in the "excellent" to "outstanding" categories of a performance evaluation.

18. **You should not overdo your job search:** Don't engage in overkill and bore everyone with your "job search" stories. Achieve balance in everything you do. Occasionally take a few days off to do nothing related to your job search. Develop a system of incentives and rewards – such as two non-job search days a week, if you accomplish targets A, B, C, and D.

19. **You should be open-minded and keep an eye open for "luck":** Too much planning can blind you to unexpected and fruitful opportunities. You should welcome serendipity. Learn to re-evaluate your goals and strategies. Seize new opportunities if appropriate.

20. **You should evaluate your progress and adjust:** Take two hours once every two weeks and evaluate your accomplishments. If necessary, tinker with your plans and reorganize your activities and priorities. Don't become too routinized and thereby kill creativity and innovation.

These principles should provide you with an initial orientation for starting your job search. As you become more experienced, you will develop your own set of operating principles that should work for you.

TIP #29
Always focus on your achievements
or accomplishments.

Your greatest assets in the eyes of employers are your achievements or accomplishments – those things you do well and result in important outcomes or benefits for employers and their organizations. Most employers are interested in two types of outcomes – saving money or making money. Whatever you do, avoid what most other job seekers do – primarily focus on their formal duties and responsibilities that normally come with a position. When writing your resume and letters and interviewing for a job, always stress your major accomplishments. Better still, try to **quantify your accomplishments**. For example, avoid stating your responsibilities in this manner:

> I was responsible for maintaining inventory for a 15-employee
> office supply store.

Instead, state your responsibilities in the form of **specific** employer-oriented accomplishments:

> Saved XYZ Company $45,000 through improved inventory
> management over an 18-month period. Installed innovative
> just-in-time ordering system that reduced returns by 50% and
> shortened delivery time by 70%.

Statistics that focus on **performance** send a powerful message to employers about your accomplishments. Whenever possible, communicate your accomplishments in such a form.

TIP #30
Position yourself as a problem solver –
someone who solves employers' problems.

Hiring is no fun. After all, employers hire individuals because they need to solve certain problems. If you communicate to employers that you are a problem solver, and you present evidence of related accom plishments, chances are you will be well received and given serious consideration for a job. Whenever possible, try to find out what

Propose solutions to an employer's problems.

specific problems an employer is encountering and come up with possible solutions that would benefit the employer. If, for example, you discover an employer's major problem is how to deal with excess ordering, you might propose a computer program you're familiar with that could streamline the ordering process and thus reduce the employer's costs.

TIP #31
Be prepared to be tested.

More and more employers subject candidates to a variety of tests as part of the screening process. These include drug screening, aptitude, and psychological tests in order to determine whether or not you fit into their organization or company. Depending on the nature of the job, some candidates may be required to take a polygraph examination. Employers also increasingly rely on situational interviews which serve as an additional test – observing how candidates actually perform job-related tasks. If you think you can just write a resume and talk your way to a new job, think again. Employer tests are here to stay and in a very big way. Try to familiarize yourself as much as possible with the types of tests employers are likely to require of you. While you may not be able to prepare for most such tests, at least be aware that you may have to take tests as a condition of employment. Make sure what you say on your resume and application as, well as in the job interview, is truthful. If not, the tests may indicate otherwise. For examples of personality tests related to employment, see Anne Hart's ***Employment Personality Tests Decoded*** (Career Press).

TIP #32
Don't lie about your past or exaggerate your future performance.

Honesty is always the best policy when conducting a job search. However, that doesn't mean you must confess your weaknesses and talk about your negatives. Focus on your strengths and accomplishments but do so truthfully. If you exaggerate your skills and lie about your background, chances are such indiscretions will eventually catch up with you, especially through background checks and testing. Since employers are looking for truthfulness, character, and value in their employees, make sure you communicate such values to employers.

TIP #33
Don't take a job that requires a long commute.

Unless you really enjoy long drives and traffic or are desperate for a job, taking a job that requires a long commute will quickly get old. Chances are you will become unhappy with the job after a few months of commuting. Try to find a job that doesn't require a long commute, or move near the job. For tips on how to quickly find a job within 30 miles of home, see Neil McNulty's and Ron Krannich's *The Quick 30/30 Job Solution* (Impact Publications).

TIP #34
Avoid jobs and employers you'll probably dislike, but be open-minded to many jobs.

Trust your intuition when it comes to identifying jobs and employers. If you feel a job or employer is not right for you, chances are it isn't. Do your research, ask questions, and learn as much as possible about jobs and employers.

There are times when you simply need to find a lifeboat job.

One of the worst things you can do is to prematurely accept a job because you're afraid you won't find a job. Take your time, consider your options, and focus on jobs and employers that best fit your interests, abilities, and skills. If you are desperate to find a job, contact a temporary employment firm or conduct a 30/30 Job Search™.

Indeed, don't pass up jobs that might lead to new opportunities as well as help you cope with your daily financial needs. There are times, especially during periods of high unemployment and personal distress, when you simply need to find a "lifeboat" job. Many of these jobs can develop into great jobs that also become wonderful careers. Neil McNulty and I outline the whys, wheres, and hows of finding lifeboat jobs in *The Quick 30/30 Job Solution.*

TIP #35
Turn potential weaknesses into strengths.

While you should recognize your weaknesses, don't let them become impediments to conducting a job search based upon your strengths. You may be able to turn some of your so-called weaknesses into strengths. For example, if you are over 50, you may feel your age is a negative. However, your age also implies you probably have a great deal of experience and good work habits. Many older workers also tend to be reliable and loyal employees. As long as you don't look for jobs geared to youth, your age may be one of your major assets. On the other hand, if you lack experience, which is often seen as a weakness, focus on entry-level jobs that require little experience. Indeed, many of these jobs are filled with individuals who are basically motivated and trainable. The fact that you have little experience may work in your favor, especially if you are intelligent, enthusiastic, and eager to learn.

TIP #36
Avoid jobs that are beneath your current salary or level of authority.

You should look for jobs that advance your career. That means finding a job that pays better than your last job and has similar or a higher level of authority and responsibility. If you seek a job that is beneath your current salary or level of authority, you will appear over-qualified, which is a red flag for many employers. They know you will probably be unhappy with the job and thus leave within a short period of time. Unless you are changing careers or have a compelling reason for seeking a job beneath your previous salary and level of authority, you will most likely become unhappy in such a job. Make sure you have a very good reason, which you can clearly explain to a prospective employer, for seeking such a job.

TIP #37
Always research the company and employer before applying for a position.

Believe it or not, some job seekers go to the job interview and ask the interviewer this killer question: *"What do you do here?"* If you want to make a very bad impression, ask that question. It indicates you didn't do your homework, and you're probably not very interested in the job – just a paycheck. That's inexcusable, especially since information on most employers is readily available on the Internet. Spend a few minutes exploring a company's website and you'll learn a great deal about the company. That information should help you target your resume and cover letter and ask intelligent questions about the company and job during the interview.

Smart job seekers know exactly whom they are dealing with when looking for a job. They research companies and employers **before** sending resumes and letters, completing applications, or going to job interviews. They tailor their resume to respond to the needs of the employer rather than send a generic resume. When they go to a job interview, they know a great deal about both the company and employer and have a list of questions prepared to ask the interviewer. These questions indicate they are interested in the job because they are well informed about the company.

3

Self-Assessment Tips

THE FIRST STEP IN ANY JOB search should be to conduct a self-assessment of your interests, skills, and abilities and relate it to specific jobs that would be most appropriate for someone with your particular strengths. You must have a very clear idea of who you are, what you do well, and what motivates you **before** you can communicate your qualifications to employers. Without this information, you are likely to wander aimlessly in the job market, going from one job to another, and engaging in a great deal of wishful thinking about what you can and will do.

A self-assessment is the **foundation** for everything else you do in your job search – goal setting, resume writing, networking, and interviewing for the job. Since it reveals who you really are in terms of specific skills, abilities, and accomplishments, a self-assessment injects realism into your job search, equips you with an important job search language, and helps you chart a clear course of action. Don't even try to write a resume or fill out a job application **before** assessing who you really are in terms of your motivated interests, skills, and abilities.

Always put yourself in the shoes of the **employer**. He or she wants to hire someone who can do the job well, get along with others, and improve operations. During the hiring process, employers want to predict the future performance of candidates based upon (1) an understanding of their past performance and (2) evidence of their motivated abilities and skills. While they can conduct background checks and administer tests, much of what they will learn about you will appear on your applications, resumes, and cover letters and be discussed during job interviews. In preparation for these activities, you will need to gather evidence of your accomplishments, give examples of your strengths, and relate stories about your achievements. The easiest way to do this is to conduct a thorough self-assessment that identifies your specific accomplishments and attendant interests and skills.

> *You need to gather evidence of your accomplishments, give examples of your strengths, and tell stories about your achievements.*

The tips I outline here should help you get your job search off and running in the right direction. If done properly, a self-assessment will save you a great deal of time and eliminate many of the frustrations associated with a job search.

TIP #38
Use a variety of approaches to identify your interests, skills, and abilities.

Some job seekers look for a magic bullet – a single test that will reveal all they need to know about themselves, from what career path to choose to the type of job that will make them happy. Indeed, career counselors often encounter such individuals who are frustrated by not knowing what to do with their lives. But there is no such magic bullet when it comes to making career choices. No single test or exercise will reveal enough information to make your job search easy. Each test or exercise looks at one or two major dimensions of human complexity. Some of these devices, for example, only focus on personality and motivation while others examine values, interests, attitudes, skills, behaviors, and aptitudes. The personality approach is by far the most popular and controversial approach.

You will find literally hundreds of career tests and exercises designed to help you clarify career choices. For job seekers, this is a bewildering world of testing because of so many alternative choices available. Many job seekers rightfully ask *"Which test or exercise is best for me?"* Our answer is very simple: No one size fits all; you need to try several different approaches.

I recommend using a variety of approaches that yield different information on yourself, from paper and pencil tests to self-directed exercises. If you do this, you will gain a great deal of information about yourself, some of which will be confirmed from one test and exercise to another. Here are some of the most popular self-assessment tests, many of which must be administered by certified career counselors and testing experts:

> *No one size (test) fits all; you need to try several different approaches.*

Personality and Motivation Tests

- California Psychological Inventory Form 434 (CPI™ 434)
- Edwards Personal Preference Schedule
- Enneagram
- Keirsey Character Sorter
- Myers-Briggs Type Indicator® (MBTI®)
- 16-Personality Factor Questionnaire (16PF)

Values Tests

- Career Beliefs Inventory (CBI)
- Minnesota Importance Questionnaire (MIQ)
- Survey of Interpersonal Values (SIV)
- Temperament and Values Inventory
- O*NET Career Values Inventory

Interests and Attitudes Tests

- Career Assessment Inventory™ – Enhanced Version (CAI-E)
- Career Exploration Inventory
- Career IQ and Interest Test (CIQIT)
- Guide to Occupational Exploration Interest Inventory

- Harrington-O'Shea Career Decision-Making System
- Jackson Vocational Interest Survey (JVIS)
- Job Search Attitude Inventory (JSAI)
- Kuder Occupational Interest Survey
- Leisure to Occupational Connection Search (LOCS)
- Ohio Vocational Interest Survey
- Self-Directed Search® (SDS)
- Strong Interest Inventory®
- Vocational Interest Inventory

Skills, Behaviors, and Aptitudes Tests

- Barriers to Employment Success Inventory
- BRIGANCE® Diagnostic Employability Skills Inventory
- Career Decision Scale
- FIRO-B®

Multiple Indicators Tests

- APTICOM
- Armed Services Vocational Battery (ASVAB)
- Assessment of Career Decision Making (ACDM)
- The Birkman Method
- CAM Computerized One-Stop
- Campbell™ Interest and Skill Survey (CISS®)
- Career Scope
- Key Educational Vocational Assessment System (KEVAS)
- Vocational Interest, Temperament, and Aptitude System (VITAS)

In addition, you should consider completing several self-directed assessment exercises which can be analyzed on your own rather than with the assistance of a career professional. Some of the most popular such exercises include:

The Skills Map (Richard Nelson Bolles)
Autobiography of Accomplishments
Success Factor Analysis (Bernard Haldane)

SIMA (System for Identifying Motivated Abilities)
(Sima International)

These and many other tests and exercises are summarized and ana-
lyzed in our companion volumes, *I Want to Do Something Else, But
I'm Not Sure What It Is* (Impact Publications) as well as in several
testing directories: *The ETS Test Collection Catalog* (Oryx Press),
Mental Measures Yearbook (University Nebraska Press), and *Tests*
(Pro-Ed).

TIP #39
Focus on understanding your motivated abilities and skills (MAS).

One of the most useful exercises many of our readers use is something
I call the "Motivated Skills Exercise." Based on Haldane's "Success
Factor Analysis," but sometimes referred to as the "System to Identify
Motivated Skills" or "Intensive Skills Exercise," this device focuses on
identifying exactly what employers are looking for – your pattern of
motivated abilities and skills (MAS). Since employers are looking for
predictable patterns of behavior, based on the trusted theory that
one's future performance is likely to resemble one's past performance,
you need to have a clear understanding of your past patterns of
behavior. But most important of all, you want to understand what
really motivates you to excel – those things you both do well and enjoy
doing. The "Motivated Skills Exercise," which I describe in detail in
I Want to Do Something Else, But I'm Not Sure What It Is,
outlines how to generate such information on yourself within a few
hours. It basically involves six steps:

1. Identify 15-20 of your major achievements.

2. Prioritize your seven most significant achievements.

3. Write a full page on each of your prioritized achievements.

4. Elaborate on your achievements by having someone
   interview you by asking "what" and "how" questions.

5. Identify patterns by examining the interviewer's notes.

6. Synthesize the information by clustering similar skills into categories.

Here's an example of how skills might be grouped into clusters, which identify certain behavioral patterns, or what I call one's motivated abilities and skills (MAS):

Synthesized Skill Clusters

Investigate/Survey/Read	Teach/Train/Drill
Inquire/Probe/Question	Perform/Show/Demonstrate
Learn/Memorize/Practice	Construct/Assemble/Put together
Evaluate/Appraise/Assess	
Compare	Organize/Structure/Provide
	definition/Plan/Chart course
Influence/Involve/Get	Strategize/Coordinate
participation/Publicize	
Promote	Create/Design/Adapt/Modify

TIP #40
Consider taking the *Myers-Briggs Type Indicator®, Self-Directed Search®*, and *Strong Interest Inventory®*

The three most popular assessment devices used in career counseling are the *Myers-Briggs Type Indicator(MBTI), Self-Directed Search (SDS)*, and *Strong Interest Inventory (SII)*. If you decide to take a few counselor-assisted tests, I highly recommend starting with these. Here's what you get:

- **Myers-Briggs Type Indicator (MBTI):** This is the most popular personality inventory in the world used by psychologists and career counselors. It has multiple applications for everything from marital counseling to executive development programs. Based on Carl Gustav Jung's theory of personality types, this simplified application of his complex theory attempts to measure personality dispositions and interests – the way people absorb information, decide, and communicate. It analyzes preferences to four dichotomies (extroversion/ introversion, sensing/intuiting, thinking/feeling, judging/perceiving) which result in 16 personality types. The MBTI comes in a variety of forms. Available through Consulting Psychologists Press (www.cpp.com and www.skillsone.com) and most colleges, universities, and testing centers.

- **Self-Directed Search (SDS):** One of the most widely used and adapted interest inventories in career counseling. Designed to assist individuals in making career choices based on an analysis of different orientations toward people, data, and things. It matches interests with six types (realistic, investigative, artistic, social, enterprising, and conventional) that are, in turn, related to different types of occupations that match these types. Used in helping determine how one's interests fit with various occupations. Influential in developing the assessment approach found in Richard Nelson Bolles's ***What Color Is Your Parachute?*** and ***What Color Is Your Parachute Workbook***. Also available in other versions, such as *Self-Directed Search Career Explorer (SDS CE)* and *Self-Directed Search Form R (SDS Form R)*. Available through Psychological Assessment Resources (www3.parinc.com).

- **Strong Interest Inventory:** Next to the *Myers-Briggs Type Indicator* and the *Self-Directed Search* , this remains one of the most popular assessment devices used by career counselors. Individuals respond to 317 multiple-choice items to determine their occupational interests according to six occupational themes, 25 interest scales, occupational scales, and personal style scales. Used extensively for career guidance, occupational decisions, employment placement, educational choices, and vocational rehabilitation programs. Available through Consulting Psychologists Press (www.cpp.com) and most schools, colleges, universities, and testing centers.

At the same time, you should supplement these paper and pencil tests with some of the self-directed assessment exercises I identified in Tips #38 and #39.

TIP #41
Contact a certified career counselor or testing expert to administer various testing instruments if necessary.

A certified career counselor can become immensely useful at various stages of your job search. But using one at the very beginning of your job search for completing and analyzing the self-assessment and testing work can be critical to all other stages of your job search. You should be able to find a certified career counselor or testing expert through your local community college or one-stop career center. The following websites also will give you information on such professionals:

- **National Board for Certified Counselors, Inc.**   www.nbcc.org

- **National Career Development Association**   www.ncda.org

- **Certified Career Coaches**   www.certifiedcareer coaches.com

- **Career Planning and Adult Development Network**   www.careernetwork.org

- **America's Service Locator**   www.servicelocator.org

TIP #42
Consult various books that include self-directed assessment tools.

Numerous books outline a large variety of assessment tools which readers can readily use in assessing their interests, skills, and abilities. Some writers only outline a single device which they claim will provide you with all the necessary career decision-making information. Many of these writers use psychological and personality approaches. Others include several devices from which you can pick and choose. Many of these books focus on measuring different types of interests, skills, and aptitudes. The following resources will give you a thorough introduction in the often bewildering world of self-assessment:

Personality Approaches

Do What You Are (Paul D. Tieger and Barbara Barron-Tieger)
I'm Not Crazy, I'm Just Not You (Roger R. Pearman and Sarah C. Albritton)
Making Vocational Choices (John Holland)
The Pathfinder (Nicholas Lore)
Personality Type: An Owner's Manual (Lenore Thomson)
Please Understand Me II (David Keirsey)
The Self-Directed Search (John Holland)
What's Your Type of Career? (Donna Dunning)
What Type Am I? (Jean Kummerow, Linda Kirby, Nancy Barger)

Individual Approaches

Beat the Odds (Martin Yate)
Discover What You're Best At (Linda Gale)
Finding Your Perfect Work (Paul and Sarah Edwards)
I Could Do Anything If Only I Knew What It Was (Barbara Sher)
I Don't Know What I Want, But I Know It's Not This (Julie Jansen)
Live the Life You Love (Barbara Sher)
Now, Discover Your Strengths (Marcus Buckingham)

Multiple Approaches

Career, Aptitude, and Selection Tests (James Barrett)
Career Tests (Louis Janda)
The Everything Career Tests Book (A. Bronwyn Llewellyn)
Guide to Occupational Exploration (Farr, Ludden, Shatkin)
I Want To Do Something Else, But I'm Not Sure What It Is (Ron and Caryl Krannich)
The Psychologist's Book of Self-Tests (Louis Janda)
Test Your Own Job Aptitude (James Barrett)

Predestination and Religious Approaches

The Crystal-Barkley Guide to Taking Charge of Your Career
  (Barkley and Sandburg)
How to Find Your Mission in Life (Richard Nelson Bolles)
The Purpose-Driven Life (Rick Warren)
The Truth About You (Arthur F. Miller and Ralph T. Mattson)
What Color Is Your Parachute? (Richard Nelson Bolles)

Positive Thinking, Story, and Dreaming Approaches

100 Ways to Motivate Yourself (Steve Chandler)
Attitude Is Everything (Keith Harrell)
Awaken the Giant Within (Anthony Robbins)
Be Happy Attitudes (Dr. Robert H. Schuller)
Change Your Attitude (Bay and Macpherson)
Change Your Thinking, Change Your Life (Brian Tracy)
Create Your Own Future (Brian Tracy)
Dream It, Do It (Sharon Cook and Graciela Sholander)
Eat That Frog! (Brian Tracy)
Focal Point (Brian Tracy)
How to Get What You Want (Zig Ziglar)
How to Win Friends and Influence People (Dale Carnegie)
Live With Passion! (Anthony Robbins)
The Magic of Thinking Big (David Schwartz)
Maximum Achievement (Brian Tracy)
Personal Power (Anthony Robbins)
The Power of Positive Thinking (Dr. Norman Vincent Peale)
Practical Dreamer's Handbook (Paul and Sarah Edwards)
Reinventing Yourself (Steve Chandler)
The Secret (Rhonda Byrne)
Secrets of Success (Og Mandino)
Six Attitudes for Winners (Dr. Norman Vincent Peale)
Success Through a Positive Mental Attitude (Napoleon Hill)
Think and Grow Rich (Napoleon Hill)
TurboCoach (Brian Tracy)
Unlimited Power (Anthony Robbins)
What Should I Do With My Life? (Po Bronson)
You Can Become the Person You Want to Be (Dr. Robert
  H. Schuller)

TIP #43
Explore several online assessment tools.

Within the past few years, several companies have developed online assessment devices which you can quickly access via the Internet 24 hours a day in the comfort of your home or office. Some tests are self-scoring and free of charge while others require interacting with a fee-based certified career counselor or testing expert. SkillsOne (www. skillsone.com), for example, is operated by the producers of the *Myers-Briggs Type Indicator* and *Strong Interest Inventory* – Consulting Psychologists Press. CareerLab (www.careerlab.com) offers one of the largest batteries of well respected assessment tools: *Campbell Interest and Skills Survey, Strong Interest Inventory, Myers-Briggs Type Indicator, 16-Personality Factors Profile, FIRO-B, California Psychological Inventory (CPI), The Birkman Method*, and *Campbell Leadership Index*. The following seven websites are well worth exploring for both free and fee-based online assessments tools:

- **SkillsOne** (Consulting Psychologists Press)   www.skillsone.com
  www.cpp-db.com
- **CareerLab.com**   www.careerlab.com
- **Self-Directed Search**   www.self-directed-search.com
- **Personality Online**   www.personalityonline.com
- **Keirsey Character Sorter**   www.keirsey.com
- **MAPP**   www.assessment.com
- **PersonalityType**   www.personalitytype.com

These 19 additional sites also include a wealth of related assessment devices that you can access online:

- **Analyze My Career**   www.analyzemycareer.com
- **Birkman Method**   www.birkman.com
- **Career Key**   www.careerkey.org
- **CareerLeader**   www.careerleader.com
- **CareerPlanner.com**   www.careerplanner.com
- **CareerPerfect.com**   www.careerperfect.com
- **Careers By Design**   www.careers-by-design.com
- **College Board**   www.myroad.com

- Enneagram   www.ennea.com
- HumanMetrics   www.humanmetrics.com
- Internet IQ Tests
  and Personality Test   www.2h.com
- Jackson Vocational
  Interest Inventory   www.jvis.com
- My Future   www.myfuture.com
- Sima International.com   www.simainternational.com
- Profiler   www.profiler.com
- QueenDom   www.queendom.com

TIP #44
Expect employers to subject you to different tests to assess your suitability for the job.

While you definitely want to assess your interests, skills, and abilities at this initial job search stage, assessment doesn't end here and with you alone. Expect employers to use a variety of tests to learn more about your interests, skills, and abilities in order to further screen you for employment. Depending on the nature of the job, you may need to take a drug test, an aptitude test, a personality test, or even a character and ethics test. Some jobs may even require a polygraph exam. As I noted in Tip #31, more and more employers are turning to such tests in order to better predict the suitability of individuals for employment. In most cases you cannot prepare for these tests.

TIP #45
Take the self-assessment information seriously in organizing all phases of your job search.

Self-assessment information can be invaluable for organizing each phase of your job search. Based on knowledge of your strengths, you should be able to develop a powerful job objective and target your job search on those jobs and employers that best coincide with your interests, skills, and abilities. However, don't become obsessed with or over-rely on such information. Many self-assessment tests and exercises generate very simplistic information that may underwhelm you. If you have a great deal of experience, you may find the *Myers-Briggs Type Indicator, Self-Directed Search, Strong Interest Inventory,* and *Motivated Skills Exercise* merely confirm what you already know about yourself. In this case, you need to get on with your job search by focusing on communicating your accomplishments to employers. Avoid the temptation of trying to be someone you are not or chasing after glamorous jobs that appeal to you but which do not relate to your foundation interests, skills, and abilities.

4

Goal and Objective Setting Tips

W HAT REALLY MOTIVATES you to do the things you do? Do you have goals that direct your actions or do you just go with the flow of things because you are too busy with life? Do you have a clear idea of what you want to be doing in another six months or even five or 10 years from now? Do you dream a lot about your future? How realistic are your dreams and goals? If you wrote your obituary today, what might it include about your achievements in life and contributions to others?

If you have a not-so-hot background, you need to pay particular attention to the quality of your goals. Always remember that **goals and objectives** are **statements of what you want to do in the future**. Chances are you either lack goals or have unrealistic goals.

Successful job seekers know what they want to do. They have goals that guide them toward a job that's fit for them. Without goals, you may wander aimlessly in the job market. Like a ship without a rudder and buffeted by changing winds, you may go in one direction and then in another, not knowing where you will eventually end up. While the future may not be predictable, it is something you can shape for yourself if you have clear goals and a plan of action. Indeed, that's my goal in this chapter – make sure you develop realistic career goals.

TIP #46
Take time to develop a powerful objective.

Many job seekers discover one of the most difficult job search tasks is to develop a job or career objective. This is not something you just create in a few minutes. A basic 25-word objective may take you two or more weeks to develop. You'll draft an initial objective and then further refine it based upon information about your strengths, em-

> *A basic 25-word objective may take two or more weeks to develop. It will become the most important element in your job search arsenal.*

ployers, and jobs. You constantly think about who you are and what you want to really achieve in the future. This process of developing an objective will clear up many fuzzy thoughts as you begin seeing the light at the end of what may initially appear to be a very long tunnel. But once you get your objective right, you'll see how important that objective is to your whole job search as well as your future. As you constantly repeat and refine your objective, you'll discover it's the single most important element in your job search arsenal. Thus, take lots of time to get this initial step right.

TIP #47
Your objective will give you certain advantages in the job market.

Identifying what it is you want to do can be one of the most difficult job search tasks. Indeed, most job hunters lack clear objectives. Many engage in a random and somewhat mindless search for jobs by identifying available job opportunities and then adjusting their skills and objectives to fit specific job openings. While you can get a job using this approach, you may be misplaced and unhappy with what you find. You will fit into a job rather than find a job that is fit for you.

Knowing what you want to do can have numerous benefits. First, you define the job market rather than let it define you. The inherent fragmentation and chaos of the job market should be advantageous for you, because it enables you to systematically organize job opportunities around your specific objectives and skills. Second, you will communicate professionalism to prospective employers. They will receive a precise indication of your interests, qualifications, and purposes, which places you ahead of most other applicants. Third, being purposeful means being able to communicate to employers what you really want to do. Employers are not interested in hiring indecisive and confused individuals who will probably have difficulty taking initiative because they really don't know what they should be doing in the first place. Employers want to know what it is you can and will do **for them**. With a clear objective – based upon a thorough understanding of your motivated skills and interests – you can take control of the situation as you demonstrate your value to prospective employers.

> *Employers do not want to hire indecisive and confused individuals. They want to know what you can and will do for them.*

Finally, few employers really know what they want in a candidate. Like most job seekers, employers often lack clear employment objectives and knowledge about how the job market operates. If you know what you want and can help the employer define his or her "needs" as your objective, you will have achieved a tremendously advantageous position in the job market.

TIP #48
Your objective should directly relate to your self-assessment information.

Your strongest goals should directly relate to your motivated abilities and skills as well as incorporate a realistic vision of your future. When combined with an assessment of your interests, values, abilities, and skills and related to specific jobs, your goals give your job search needed direction and meaning for the purpose of targeting specific employers.

Without goals, your job search may founder as you present an image of uncertainty and confusion to potential employers. When you identify your strengths, you also create the necessary database and vocabulary for developing your job objective. Using this vocabulary, you should be able to communicate your strengths to prospective employers. If you fail to do the preliminary self-assessment work necessary for developing a clear objective, you will probably meander through a highly decentralized, fragmented, and chaotic job market looking for interesting jobs you might fit into. Your goal, instead, should be to find a job or career that is compatible with your interests, motivations, skills, and talents as well as related to a vision of your future.

> *When you identify your strengths, you create the necessary database and vocabulary for developing your job objective.*

TIP #49
A job or career objective is not the same as a mission statement.

A job or career objective states what you want to do in the future and is related to both your strengths and the needs of employers. A mission statement is usually associated with the kind of person you would like to become and often has spiritual or religious tones. It focuses on your purpose or significance in life. If you want to develop a mission statement, the quickest way to do this is to write your obituary, which will generate a statement of how you would like to be remembered after death. For assistance in developing a mission statement, read Stephen Covey's *7 Habits of Highly Effective People* (Warner Books) and Richard Nelson Bolles's *How to Find Your Mission in Life* (Ten Speed Press). For assistance in writing a job or career objective, see my *High Impact Resumes and Letters*, *I Want to Do Something Else But I'm Not Sure What It Is*, and *Change Your Job, Change Your Life*, (Impact Publications). See the order form at the end of this book.

TIP #50
Relate your objective to both your interests and the employer's needs.

Your objective should communicate that you are a **purposeful individual who achieves results**. It can be stated over different time periods as well as at various levels of abstraction and specificity. You can identify short, intermediate, and long-range objectives and very general to very specific objectives. Whatever the case, it is best to know your prospective audience before deciding on the type of objective. Your objective should reflect your career interests as well as employers' needs. Examples of different types of objectives at different levels are included in Tip #54.

TIP #51
Your objective should be realistic.

Objectives should be **realistic**. For example, you may want to become president of the United States or solve all the world's problems. However, these objectives are probably unrealistic. While they may represent your ideals, dreams, and fantasies, you need to be more realistic in terms of what you can personally accomplish in the immediate future given your particular skills, pattern of accomplishments, level of experience, and familiarity with the job market. What, for example, are you prepared to deliver to prospective employers over the next few months? While it is good to set challenging goals, you can overdo it. Refine your objective by thinking about the next major step or two you would like to make in your career advancement. Develop a realistic action plan that focuses on the details of progressing your career one step at a time. Such a plan will allow you to experience success – a key motivator for advancing your career. If you have unrealistic goals, you are likely to experience failure and thus become depressed at being a "loser." By all means avoid making a grandiose leap outside reality!

TIP #52
Your objective should be employer-centered rather than self-centered.

Your objective should be a concise statement of what you want to do and what you have to offer to an employer. The position you seek is "what you want to do"; your qualifications are "what you have to offer." Your objective should state your **strongest qualifications** for meeting employers' needs. It should communicate what you have to offer an employer without empha-sizing what you expect the employer to do for you. In other words, your objective should be **work-centered**, not self-centered; it should not contain trite terms which emphasize what you want, such as give me a(n) "opportunity for advancement," "position working with people," "progressive company," or "creative position." Such terms are viewed as "canned" job search language which says little of value about you. Above all, your objective should reflect your honesty and integrity; it should not be "hyped."

> *Your objective should be a concise statement of what you want to do and what you have to offer to an employer.*

TIP #53
Always include an objective on your resume.

One of the most controversial debates among job seekers and career professionals concerns whether or not to include an objective on your resume. One group argues it's not necessary to include an objective on the resume because (1) it locks you into one type of job, (2) most objectives are trite and thus may diminish your candidacy, and (3) it's best to include an objective in your cover letter. I belong to the second group that argues for **always** including an objective on your resume. My reasons are quite simple. First, research indicates that employers prefer seeing objectives on resumes. In fact, an objective is one of the most important things employers look for on a resume! Second, an objective indicates you are a **purposeful individual** who knows what you want to achieve in the future; employers want to hire such goal-oriented individuals. Third, and perhaps most important of all, an objective becomes the **central organizing principle** for including other items on the resume; indeed, every element included on the resume should flow directly from the objective. Fourth, an objective stated in the form of skills and outcomes is anything but trite; it's a powerful statement of where you and the employer will be going together in the future. Fifth, a resume without an objective often tends to be disorganized and thus requires readers to interpret what he

thinks the person wants. If an employer has to ask this question after reading your resume, you're in trouble: What does this person want to do other than land this position and a paycheck? Don't misunderstand us. People do get interviews with resumes that do not include objectives. In fact, many people get jobs without writing a resume. Our point is that you should always put your best

> *An objective becomes the central organizing principle for including other items on your resume.*

foot forward by creating the **very best resume** possible. Include an intelligent objective on your resume and you will be communicating your **best self** to employers. Leave it off your resume and you will diminish your candidacy and force the reader to speculate about what you really want to do in the future.

TIP #54
Avoid putting a trite objective on your resume.

One of the major reasons some resume writing experts oppose putting an objective on a resume is because they have encountered so many trite objectives. Take, for example, these two objectives:

Objective #1

Retail Management position with an opportunity for advancement.

Objective #2

Retail Management position which will use sales/customer service experience and creative abilities for innovative product display and merchandising. Long term goal: Become merchandise manager with corporate-wide responsibilities for product line.

The first one is a typical trite objective that basically says nothing. Worst of all, it's a very self-centered objective – the individual wants a job that enables him or her to get ahead. On the other hand, the second objective stresses key interests and skills as well as focuses on the employer's needs.

The best type of objective is oriented toward **skills and results**. It follows this format:

I would like a job where I can use my ability to _____, which will result in _____.

For example, at a general level, an objective that follows this format might be stated as follows:

I would like a job where my experience in retail management, supported by strong sales/customer service experience, will result in excellent product displays and merchandising.

As noted in our example above (Objective #2), this general objective should be restated on a resume as a job-targeted objective:

Retail Management position which will use sales/customer service experience and creative abilities for innovative product display and merchandising. Long term goal: Become merchandise manager with corporate-wide responsibilities for product line.

TIP #55
Make your objective the central organizing principle for implementing your job search.

Your objective should not be limited to just a section on your resume. It should be all encompassing, guiding each phase of your job search. Once you develop a powerful objective, you'll find that all of your other job search activities will fall in place as you focus laser-like on what's most important in your job search in order to achieve your goal. Without such an objective, you may have difficulty deciding what's really important to your job search and thus founder aimlessly in search of jobs that seem interesting to you but which may not relate to your major strengths.

5

Research and Information Tips

ESEARCH IS THE PROCESS of acquiring information in order to make better informed decisions. The old adage that "knowledge is power" is especially true when conducting a job search. Indeed, gathering, processing, and using information is the lifeblood of any job search.

Research should play a **central role** throughout your job search. Since you will be dealing with many individuals and organizations, you need to develop an information strategy to acquire data about, as well as gain access to, those individuals and organizations that will play the most important role in your job search. If you are interested in moving to another community, you also need to do community-based research on everything from the cost of living and housing to education and culture. The quality of information you gather and analyze should play a critical role in four major job search steps – resume and letter writing, networking, interviewing, and negotiating terms of employment.

The following tips stress how to best focus your research activities throughout your job search. Taken together, they offer a primer on job search research. Whatever you do, make sure you develop a well focused research campaign that keeps you motivated and your job search on target. In the process of doing so, you will encounter that wonderful experience called **serendipity** – chance occurrences that often result in new and productive leads.

TIP #56
Make research a central and daily activity throughout your job search.

As I indicated in the job search organizational chart in Tip #3, research should play a central and ongoing role throughout each phase of your job search. It should begin on day one and end once you receive a job offer and negotiate salary and terms of employment. Research will keep your job search fresh and focused as well as keep you energetic and motivated as you discover new people, jobs, and organizations. Best of all, research often results in many serendipitous experiences that challenge preconceived notions, alter plans, and point you in new and fruitful directions. Indeed, many job seekers land terrific jobs which they attribute to the quality of their research activities. Their research puts them in the right place at the right time to take advantage of chance occurrences that became new opportunities. When you conduct re-search and network (see Chapter 9) at the same time, you plant seeds that may quickly result in a new harvest of contacts, job leads, and invitations to job interviews.

> *Research will keep your job search fresh and focused as well as keep you energetic and motivated.*

TIP #57
Use the Internet and telephone for much of your research.

If you use the Internet for only one thing, make sure it's research. The Internet is a wonderful information and communication tool that has both strengths and weaknesses. Its major strengths for job seekers are gathering information (research) and communicating (email). As I previously noted in Tips #8 and #43, there are both proper and improper ways of using the Internet in one's job search. While few job seekers find jobs on the Internet, most could benefit enormously if they used the Internet for research, networking, and advice. Using the Internet, you can quickly research jobs, individuals, companies, and communities. Some of the best job search information can be found on the websites of employers. Be sure to explore such websites in order to learn about jobs, individuals, and organizations.

You should also use the telephone a great deal in conducting research. However, most people dislike making cold calls and leaving voicemail messages, essential actions for gathering useful information and getting job interviews. Accordingly, people who are reluctant to pick up the telephone to contact strangers are at a distinct disadvantage in today's job market. If you have difficulty making cold calls and using voicemail, be sure to read Neil McNulty's and Ron Krannich's *The Quick 30/30 Job Solution* (Impact Publications), Stephen Schiffman's *Cold Calling Techniques* (Adams Media), and Keith Rosen's *The Complete Idiot's Guide to Cold Calling* (Alpha Books). While the latter two books primarily offer useful tips on how to best use the telephone in making sales calls, their general principles are applicable to conducting research and networking relevant to a job search. My networking approaches in Chapter 9 also help individuals who are reluctant to contact strangers by phone or in person.

> *People who are reluctant to pick up the telephone to contact strangers are at a distinct disadvantage in today's job market.*

TIP #58
Investigate alternative jobs and careers.

If you are first entering the job market, re-entering after a lengthy absence, or planning to change jobs or careers, you are well advised to conduct research on alternative jobs and careers related to your interests and skills. You'll find numerous online and print resources to help you conduct such research. I highly recommend starting with the U.S. Department of Labor's bi-annual *Occupational Outlook Handbook* which profiles nearly 300 major jobs that constitute over 85 percent of all occupations in the United States. This book also can be accessed online through this URL:

www.bls.gov/oco

Other useful online career exploration resources are the O*NET and America's CareerInfoNet:

www.onetcenter.org
www.acinet.org

McGraw-Hill publishes over 250 career exploration books in three major series in such titles as *Careers in Health Care, Careers for Computer Buffs*, and *Opportunities in Interior Design and Decorating*. Facts on File publishes the *Encyclopedia of Careers and Vocational Guidance, Ferguson Career Resource Guide for Women and Minorities, 25 Jobs That Have It All, 50 Cutting Edge Jobs, Quick Prep Careers*, and several titles in the "Career Opportunities Series," such as *Career Opportunities in Forensic Science* and *Career Opportunities in Energy*. JIST Publishing includes such titles as the *Guide to Occupational Exploration, O*NET Dictionary of Occupational Titles, Top 100 Careers for College Graduates*, and *Top 100 Computer and Technical Careers*. I also publish *Jobs for Travel Lovers, The Best Jobs for the 21ˢᵗ Century, America's Top 101 Jobs for People Without a Four-Year Degree, America's Top Jobs for People Re-Entering the Workforce*, and *Best Jobs for Ex-Offenders*. Most of these books summarize alternative jobs and careers in terms of working conditions, educational and training requirements, salaries, and prospects for the future. If you are unable to find these books in your local library or bookstores, they can be ordered directly from Impact Publications by completing the order form at the end of this book or by visiting the "Career Exploration" section of Impact's online career bookstore: www.impactpublications.com.

You might also want to contact a career professional who can recommend tests that link your interests to specific jobs and careers. I explore such professionals and linkages in *I Want to Do Something Else, But I'm Not Sure What It Is* (Impact Publications).

TIP #59

Consult the right resources for uncovering information on specific organizations or companies.

You also should identify specific organizations which you are interested in learning more about. Next, compile lists of names, addresses, and telephone numbers of important individuals in each organization. Also, explore the home pages of various companies on the Internet and write or telephone them for information, such as an annual report and recruiting literature; this information may be downloadable.

The most important information you should be gathering concerns the organizations' goals, structures, functions, problems, and projected future opportunities and development. Since you invest part of your life in such organizations, treat them as you would a stock market investment. Compare and evaluate different organizations.

Several directories will assist you in researching organizations. Most are available in the reference sections of libraries or available online:

- *Almanac of American Employers*
- *Directory of American Firms Operating in Foreign Countries*
- *The Directory of Corporate Affiliations: Who Owns Whom*
- *Dun & Bradstreet's Million Dollar Directory*
- *Dun & Bradstreet's Reference Book of Corporate Managements*
- *Encyclopedia of Business Information Sources*
- *Fitch's Corporation Reports*
- *MacRae's Blue Book*
- *Moody's Manuals*
- *The Multinational Marketing and Employment Directory*
- *Standard & Poor's 500 Index*
- *Standard Rate and Data Business Publications Directory*
- *Thomas' Register of American Manufacturers*

Numerous websites will give you access to thousands of companies and organizations:

▪ CEO Express	www.ceoexpress.com
▪ Hoover's Online	www.hoovers.com
▪ Dun and Bradstreet's Million Dollar Database	www.dnbmdd.com/mddi
▪ Corporate Information	www.corporateinformation.com
▪ BizTech Network	www.brint.com
▪ AllBusiness	www.allbusiness.com
▪ BizWeb	www.bizweb.com
▪ Business.com	www.business.com
▪ America's CareerInfoNet	www.acinet.org
▪ Annual Report Service	www.annualreportservice.com
▪ Bloomberg	www.bloomberg.com
▪ Chamber of Commerce	www.chamberof commerce.com
▪ CNN Money	http//money.cnn.com
▪ Daily Stocks	www.dailystocks.com
▪ The Corporate Library	www.thecorporatelibrary.com
▪ Forbes Lists	www.forbes.com/lists
▪ Fortune 500	www.fortune.com
▪ Harris InfoSource	www.harrisinfo.com
▪ Inc. 500	www.inc.com/500
▪ Moodys	www.moodys.com
▪ Motley Fool	www.fool.com
▪ NASDAQ	www.nasdaq.com
▪ OneSource	www.onesource.com
▪ Standard & Poors	www2.standardandpoors.com
▪ The Street	www.thestreet.com
▪ ThomasNet	www.thomasnet.com

I consider the first five websites to be the top ones for conducting research on companies and organizations.

If you are interested in a job with a particular organization, you should visit their website for employment information and/or contact the human resources office for information on the types of jobs offered within the organization. Many companies include an extensive and relatively sophisticated employment section on their homepage that allows individuals to enter their resumes into a company database or apply online for specific positions. Indeed, companies are increasingly recruiting online for all types of positions, from entry level to top management. Examples include Cisco Systems (www.cisco.com), Motorola (www.motorola.com), Microsoft (www.microsoft.com), and the Boston Consulting Group (www.bcg.com). You may be able to examine vacancy announcements which describe the duties and responsibilities of specific jobs as well as survey the profiles of key company personnel. Some companies even include information about the company culture and tips on conducting an effective job search with the company! If you are interested in working for federal, state, or local governments, each agency will have a personnel office which can supply you with descriptions of available jobs. To gain quick Internet access to **federal government** agencies, including vacancy announcements, go to the following websites:

- FedWorld   www.fedworld.gov
- USA Jobs   www.usajobs.com
- FederalJobs   www.fedjobs.com
- Federal Jobs Digest   www.jobsfed.com

If you wish to work in **law enforcement**, visit these websites:

- LawEnforcementJobs   www.lawenforcementjobs.com
- PoliceEmployment.com   www.policeemployment.com
- JobCop.com   www.jobcop.com
- 911 HotJobs   www.911hotjobs.com
- Officer.com   www.officer.com/jobs
- Blueline.com   www.theblueline.com

Individuals oriented toward working in the **nonprofit sector** should visit these useful gateway websites:

- GuideStar   www2.guidestar.org
- Action Without Borders   www.idealist.org
- Foundation Center   http://.foundationcenter.org
- Independent Sector   www.independentsector.org

TIP #60
Contact people who can provide useful information.

While examining websites and directories and reading books on alternative jobs and careers will provide you with useful job search information, much of this material may be too general for specifying the right job for you. In the end, the best information will come directly from people in specific jobs in specific organizations. To get this information you must **interview people**. You especially want to learn more about the people who make the hiring decisions.

You especially want to learn more about the people who make the hiring decisions.

You might begin your investigations by contacting various professional and trade associations for detailed information on jobs and careers relevant to their members. Since most of these organizations have homepages on the Internet, you should be able to locate their websites by using one of the standard search engines, such as www.google.com and www.yahoo.com, or by visiting these two gateway websites to trade and professional associations:

- **Associations on the Net**   www.ipl.org/ref/AON
- **ASAE**   www.asaecenter.org

For names, addresses, telephone numbers, websites, emails, and publications of such associations, consult the following key directories, which are available in most libraries:

- *Associations USA* (Omnigraphics)
- *The Encyclopedia of Associations* (Gale Cengage)
- *National Trade and Professional Associations* (Columbia Books)

Your most productive research activity will be **talking** to people or **networking** for information, advice, and referrals. Informal, word-of-mouth communication is still the most effective channel of job search information. In contrast to reading books or exploring the Internet, you can get more current, detailed, and accurate information from **people**. Ask them about:

- Occupational fields
- Job requirements and training
- Interpersonal environments
- Performance expectations
- Their problems
- Salaries
- Advancement opportunities
- Future growth potential of the organization
- How to acquire more information and contacts in a particular field

You may be surprised how willingly friends, acquaintances, and even strangers offer useful information. But before you talk to people, do your research so that you are better able to ask thoughtful questions.

TIP #61
Ask the right questions of the
right people.

The quality of your research will only be as good as the questions you ask. Therefore, you should focus on a few key questions that will yield useful information for guiding your job search. Answers to these questions will help make important job search decisions relevant to informational and job interviews.

Who Has the Power to Hire?

Finding out who has the power to hire may take some research effort on your part. Keep in mind that human resources offices normally do not have the power to hire. They handle much of the paperwork involved in announcing vacancies, taking applications, testing candidates, screening credentials, and placing new employees on the payroll. In other words, personnel offices tend to perform auxiliary support functions for those who do the actual hiring – usually individuals in operating units.

If you want to learn who really has the power to hire, you need to conduct research on the particular organization that interests you. You should ask specific questions concerning who normally is responsible for various parts of the hiring process:

- Who describes the positions?
- Who announces vacancies?
- Who receives applications?
- Who administers tests?
- Who selects eligible candidates?
- Who chooses whom to interview?
- Who conducts the interview?
- Who offers the jobs?

If you ask these questions about a specific position you will quickly identify who has what powers to hire. Chances are the power to hire is **shared** between the human resources office and the operating unit. You should not neglect the personnel office, and in some cases it will play a powerful role in all aspects of the hiring. Your research will reveal to what degree the hiring function is centralized, decentralized, or fragmented within a particular organization.

How Does Organization X Operate?

It's best to know as much as possible about the internal operations of an organization before joining it. Your research may uncover information that would convince you that an organization is not one in which you wish to invest your time and effort. You may learn, for example, that Company X has a history of terminating employees before they become vested in the company retirement system. Or Company X may be experiencing serious financial problems and morale may be extremely low. They may lie to their employees or engage in unethical behavior. Or advancement within Company X may be very political, and company politics are vicious and debilitating.

You can get financial information about most companies by examining their annual reports as well as by talking to individuals who know the organization well. Information on the internal operations, especially company politics and power, must come from individuals who work within the organization. Ask them: *"Is this a good organization to work for?"* and let them expand on specific areas you wish to probe – advancement opportunities, working conditions, relationships among co-workers and supervisors, growth patterns, internal politics, management style, work values, and opportunities for taking initiative.

What Do I Need to Do to Get a Job With Organization X?

The best way to find how to get a job in a particular organization is to follow the advice in the next chapter on prospecting, networking, and informational interviewing. This question can only be answered by talking to people who know both the formal and informal hiring practices.

You can get information on the formal hiring system by visiting the company's website or contacting the human resources office. A telephone call should be sufficient for this information.

But you must go beyond the formal system and human resources office in order to learn how best to conduct your job search. This means contacting people who know how one really gets hired in the organization, which may or may not follow the formal procedures. The best sources of information will be individuals who play a major role in the hiring process.

TIP #62
Investigate alternative communities.

Your final research target is central to all other research targets and it may occur at any stage in your research. Identifying the geographical area where you would like to work will be one of your most important decisions. Once you make this decision, other job search decisions and activities become easier. For example, if you live in a small town, you may need to move in order to change careers. If you are a member of a two-career family, opportunities for both you and your spouse will be greater in a growing metropolitan area. If you decide to move to another community, you will need to develop a long-distance job search campaign which has different characteristics from a local campaign. It involves visiting community websites, writing letters, making long-distance phone calls, and visiting a community for strategic one- to two-week periods during your vacations.

Deciding where you want to live involves researching various communities and comparing advantages and disadvantages of each. In addition to identifying specific job alternatives, organizations, and individuals in the community, you need to do research on other aspects of the community. After all, you will live in the community, buy or rent a residence, perhaps send children to school, and participate in community organizations and events. Often these environmental factors are just as important to your happiness and well-being as the particular job you accept. For example, you may be leaving a $45,000 a year job for a position in your favorite community – San Francisco. But you may quickly find you are worse off with your new $60,000 a year job, because you must pay $700,000 for a home in San Francisco that is nearly identical to the $250,000 home in your small town community. Consequently, it would be foolish for you to take a new job without first researching several facets of the community other than job opportunities.

Research on different communities can be initiated from your local library or on your personal computer, if you have an Internet connection. While most of this research will be historical in nature, several resources will provide you with a current profile of various communities. Statistical overviews and comparisons of states and cities are found in the ***U.S. Census Data, The Book for the States,*** and ***The Municipal Yearbook.*** Many libraries have a reference section of telephone books on various cities. If this section is weak or absent in your local library, check out several websites that function as telephone directories, such as:

- **Switchboard**   www.switchboard.com
- **Superpages**   www.superpages.com
- **Whitepages**   www.whitepages.com
- **Yellow Pages**   www.yellow.com
- **Yahoo Yellow Pages** http://yp.yahoo.com

In addition to giving you names, addresses, and telephone numbers, the Yellow Pages are invaluable sources of information on the specialized structures of the public and private sectors of individual communities. The library may also have state and community directories as well as subscriptions to some state and community magazines and city newspapers. Be sure to explore the many newspapers and magazines linked to this rich set of websites:

■ **Internet Public Library**	www.ipl.org/div/news
■ **NewsDirectory.com**	http://newsdirectory.com
■ **Newslink**	www.newslink.org
■ **Newspapers.com**	www.newspapers.com
■ **Online Newspapers**	www.onlinenewspapers.com
■ **The Paper Boy**	www.thepaperboy.com
■ **CEO Express**	www.ceoexpress.com

Research magazine, journal, and newspaper articles on different communities by consulting several print and online references available through your local library.

The Internet has a wealth of information on the best places to live and work. For data and perspectives on the best places to live, visit these websites:

■ **Sperling's BestPlaces**	www.bestplaces.net
■ **Find Your Spot**	www.findyourspot.com
■ **Kid Friendly Cities**	www.kidfriendlycities.org
■ **Money Magazine**	www.money.cnn.com/best/bplive
■ **Relocate America**	http://top100.relocate-america.com

For the best places to work, check out these websites:

■ **Bestplacestowork.org** (government)	www.bestplacestowork.org
■ **CollegeGrad.com**	www.collegegrad.com/top employers
■ **EmploymentSpot**	www.employmentspot.com/top-lists
■ **Forbes Magazine**	www.forbes.com/lists
■ **Fortune Magazine**	www.fortune.com ("Rankings")
■ **Great Place to Work**	http://greatplacetowork.com
■ **JobStar Central**	http://jobstar.org/hidden/bestcos.php

- Quintessential Careers   www.quintcareers.com/
                            best_places_to_work.html
- Working Mother   www.workingmother.com
                            ("Best Companies")

If you want to explore various communities, you should examine several of these gateway community sites:

- AOL CityGuide   http://digitalcity.com
- Boulevards   www.boulevards.com
- Cities.com   www.cities.com
- City Travel Guide http://citytravelguide.com
- Insiders' Guide   http://insiders.com
- TOWD   www.towd.com
- USA City Link   http://usacitylink.com

Several relocation websites also provide a wealth of information on communities. Check these sites out for linkages to major communities:

- Homefair.com   www.homefair.com
- RelocationCentral http://relocationcentral.com
- Runzheimer   www.runzheimer.com

Most major communities and newspapers have websites, where you'll find a wealth of community-based information and linkages, from newspapers and housing information to local employers, schools, recreation, and community services. If you don't have Internet access, check with your local library. Most libraries have computers connected to the Internet for use by their patrons. Several employment sites include relocation information and salary calculators which provide information on the cost of living in, as well as the cost of moving to, different communities.

If you are trying to determine the best place to live, you should start with the latest edition of Bert Sperling's and Peter Sander's **Cities Ranked and Rated** and David Savageau's **Places Rated Almanac** (John Wiley & Sons). These books rank cities by various indicators. Both *Money* magazine and *U.S. News & World Report* publish annual surveys of the best places to live in the U.S.

Andrea Kay's *Greener Pastures: How to Find a Job in Another Place* (St. Martin's) outlines useful strategies for conducting a long-distance job search campaign, including the emotional and financial challenges.

You should also consult several city job banks that will give you contact information on specific employers in major metropolitan communities. Adams Media regularly publishes *The National Job Bank* and *The JobBank Guide to Employment Services* as well as several annual job bank guides, which may or may not continue being updated. Some of the most popular titles include:

- *The Atlanta JobBank*
- *The Austin/San Antonio JobBank*
- *The Boston JobBank*
- *The Chicago JobBank*
- *The Dallas/Fort Worth JobBank*
- *The Denver JobBank*
- *The Florida JobBank*
- *The Houston JobBank*
- *The Las Vegas JobBank*
- *The Los Angeles JobBank*
- *The Minneapolis/St. Paul JobBank*
- *The New Jersey JobBank*
- *The New York JobBank*
- *The Ohio JobBank*
- *The Philadelphia JobBank*
- *The Pittsburgh JobBank*
- *The Portland JobBank*
- *The Salt Lake City JobBank*
- *The San Francisco JobBank*
- *The Seattle JobBank*
- *The Upstate New York JobBank*
- *The Virginia JobBank*
- *The Washington D.C. JobBank*
- *The Wisconsin JobBank*

After narrowing the number of communities that interest you, further research them in depth. Start by exploring community websites on the Internet (search by name of city or town). Then kick off community-based research. Ask your relatives, friends, and acquaintances for contacts in the particular community; they may know people whom you can write, telephone, or email for information and referrals. Once you have decided to focus on one community, visit it in order to establish personal contacts with key reference points, such as the local Chamber of Commerce, real estate firms, schools, libraries, churches, 40-Plus Club (if appropriate), government agencies, and business firms and associations. Begin developing personal networks based upon the research. Subscribe to the paper or electronic versions of local newspaper and to any community magazines which help profile the community. Follow the help-wanted, society, financial, and real estate sections of the newspaper – especially the Sunday edition. Keep a list of names of individuals who appear to hold influential community positions; you may want to contact them for referrals. Write letters to set up informational interviews with key people; give yourself two months of lead time to complete your letter writing campaign. Your overall research should focus on developing personal contacts which may assist you in both your job search and your move to the community.

6

Job Application Tips

MANY JOBS REQUIRE A JOB application in lieu of a resume. While once primarily designed for blue-collar and low-paying white collar positions, applications are increasingly being required by employers as an initial screening step in the hiring process. Today, many applicants also are asked to complete an online profile or mini resume which, in effect, is an application form that can be easily scanned into a company's database. Employers prefer using such profiles because they standardize the information received from candidates and make it much easier to assess qualifications.

But completing a job application or online profile is by no means a simple fill-in-the-blanks writing or typing exercise. Like writing resumes and letters, you need to carefully assess each section, select appropriate language, and be as truthful and forthcoming as possible without being stupid. Keeping in mind our earlier discussion of self assessment in Chapter 3, always focus on your strengths and project an image of competence and predictability. In the end, employers want to hire individuals they like – ones they can relate well to and who can do the job well. Your application should communicate the right combination of employer-oriented values.

TIP #63
Prepare to complete each section
of a job application.

You are expected to complete each section of a job application and respond to each question. Unless you have serious red flags in your background, avoid leaving blanks, since no response may raise red flags in the eyes of the employer – you lack attention to detail or you may be hiding something. If you decide not to respond to a question because it doesn't pertain to your situation, write "N/A" (not applicable). If you do not wish to respond in detail to a question because your response may be misinterpreted and thus raise red flags, include a short statement, such as "Will discuss at the appropriate time" or "Please contact for details" or just leave it blank. However, an application that includes blanks leaves the reader to wonder "Why didn't he respond to this question? Is there some problem here?" But if

> *Avoid leaving blanks, since no response may raise red flags in the eyes of the employer.*

you do write something, the content of what you say may be worse than leaving it bank. It's your call what to do in this situation.

TIP #64
Answer all questions as completely
as possible.

Too often job seekers think the purpose of an application is to document their employment history, provide information on salary history, and include a list of references. Yes and no. The person reviewing your application has many concerns that go far beyond a historical record of employment. The individual is primarily trying to screen you out of consideration. The art of handling job applications includes reading between the lines by looking for skills, interests, and anything negative that could knock you out of the competition. Indeed, like resumes, applications can be very revealing of possible red flags – you admit to a criminal conviction, you reveal being fired, you have little experience, your previous jobs do not relate to the position in question, your salary history or requirements are too high or too low, you include a strange mix of references that do not relate to previous employment. Given the space available, try to provide as much positive information about yourself as possible. When asked about your employment history, include the employer's name, your job title, inclusive employment dates, and a brief statement of your accomplishments, similar to

> *The person reviewing your application is primarily trying to screen you out of consideration.*

what would normally appear on an outstanding resume. However, be careful in providing too much information that may distract from your central qualifications, such as any negative reasons why you left previous positions. Always keep in mind the central purpose of completing an application – to get an invitation to a job interview. Like a resume, your application should become an advertisement to interview you for a job. Be complete, but provide just enough information to persuade the reader to contact you for an interview.

TIP #65
Select your references carefully.

Since employers increasingly check references, be sure to include a set of references that is very supportive of your candidacy. Most of your references should relate to your previous employment. They should be able to tell a prospective employer that you have the skills, abilities, and energy to do the job and give examples of your accomplishments and how you work with others. You need to do two things in regards to references. First, prepare your references for your job search by contacting them ahead of time. Inform them of your employment interests and ask if they would be willing to give you a positive recommendation. If you have a resume, send them a copy so they will remember who you are in terms of education, employment, interests, and skills. Second, select a combination of both professional and personal references. One individual should be able to vouch for your character and personality. This person could be a former teacher, a minister, or a colleague. Avoid including self-serving references, such as a relative or close friend. You don't want a reference checker to call such individuals and ask their relationships to you and discover they are your parent, uncle, or your close friend. Such individuals do not add value to your candidacy. Third, prepare a list of references, including the name, address, telephone number, and email address, and take that list with you to the place where you will be completing the application. You don't want to be caught off guard and not have this information at hand when asked to fill out an application.

> *Most references should relate to your previous employment. Avoid including self-serving references, such as a relative or close friend.*

TIP #66
Handle sensitive red flag questions honestly and tactfully.

Three sections on most applications require sensitivity and discretion on your part since your answers could raise red flags that would knock you out of further consideration.

First, consider how you would respond to the standard question about whether you have ever been **convicted of a crime or a felony**. If you have, your choices are to lie and say "No," confess by saying "Yes" and explaining your conviction, or leave the question blank. Whatever you do, don't lie; your red flag will most likely show up on a background check and will be legitimate grounds for firing. If you acknowledge a conviction and are asked to give details, note that you will discuss this matter at the appropriate time, which is during a job interview. If you leave this question blank, you may be asked to explain your non-response at the time of an interview, either a telephone screening or an actual job interview. Since it is always best to explain your situation at the job interview, you are better off leaving this question blank and first get invited to the interview. If you say

"Yes" and try to explain your conviction in writing on the application, you will likely have a big red flag that will not go away regardless of your explanation.

Second, if asked about your **employment history and reasons for leaving**, be careful what you say, especially if you were fired or unhappy with your employer. Candor in this situation can work against you, especially if you use the word "fired" or "terminated." Either leave this section blank or use the universal career transition phrases "sought a new opportunity" or "career advancement," which indeed you did.

> *Whatever you do, don't lie; your red flag will most likely show up on a background check and will be legitimate grounds for firing.*

Third, if asked to state your **salary history or salary requirements**, be very careful how you answer this question. In the case of salary history, state a range that would include your base salary plus other compensation, which can run an additional 40 percent over your base salary. For example, if you received a $40,000 base salary on your last job, you may learn you also received an additional $20,000 in benefits. Therefore, your salary history in this case could be stated as $40,000 - $60,000.

In the case of salary expectations, you may want to immediately screen yourself in or out by stating a figure. However, if you want to stay in the running it's best to give a salary range rather than a specific figure. Better still, write "Negotiable," since salary is something you want to negotiate. In fact, you need to learn more about the position, and the employer needs to learn more about you before you can discuss salary. If you state a figure or even a range at this stage, you begin to reveal your hand. The employer knows exactly where you are coming from in terms of salary expectations. If you are too high, you'll be immediately knocked out of consideration for a job interview. If you are too low, you may not have much value in the eyes of the employer. You need to get to the interview and then persuade the employer to reveal his hand first by letting you know what he normally pays someone with your qualifications.

TIP #67
Attach an achievement-oriented resume if appropriate.

An application or online resume form gives the employer the advantage – he forces you to present your qualifications according to his categories. On the other hand, a resume gives the job seeker the advantage since it forces the employer to examine qualifications according to the applicant's categories. If you have developed an achievement-oriented resume that includes your objective and stresses your skills and accomplishments, do attach it to your application. Two of the most powerful sections on your resume – objective and accomplishments – normally do not appear on an application. When you attach such a resume to your application, you should be able to greatly enhance your qualifications in the eyes of employers. Your resume gives your application added value and places you at an advantage compared to other applicants.

TIP #68
Ask about the selection process and hiring decision.

Once you complete your application and give it to the employer, be sure to ask about the selection process. When, for example, do they expect to start interviewing candidates and making a hiring decision? Would it be okay for you to check back with the employer on the status of your application? When you ask these questions, you open the door to conducting a critical follow-up.

TIP #69
Follow up your application with a telephone call.

Be sure to follow up your application with a telephone call. You should do this within five days of submitting your application. When you call, your conversation should go something like this:

Hi, this is James Olsen. Last week I submitted my application for the inventory management position. I'm calling to see if you have any questions as well as inquire if we could meet to discuss how my skills and experience can best meet your needs. Would it be possible to set up an interview next week?

While this follow-up call may seem somewhat aggressive, keep in mind three things related to your phone call. First, you may be competing with dozens of applicants who do not make such a follow-up call. As a result, you stand out from the crowd, which is something you want to do. Second, your call indicates both initiative and interest in the job; many employers appreciate encountering such candidates. Third, you have nothing to lose and everything to gain by asking for an interview. If the response is that they will call if they wish to interview you, then ask when you might hear from them and when they expect to make a hiring decision. Try to get as much information as possible on the hiring process.

Always end the conversation by indicating your continuing interest in the position and thanking them for the opportunity to apply for the position. Get the person's name and follow up with a thank-you letter which indicates your continuing interest in the position and expressing your thanks for the information and their consideration. Such a thank-you note communicates one of the most important values in the hiring process – you are truly interested in the position and you are a very thoughtful individual. Employers like to hire such people.

7

Resume Writing, Distribution, and Follow-Up Tips

YOUR RESUME WILL BE your most important calling card for getting job interviews that hopefully will lead to job offers and a satisfying job. However, writing, producing, distributing, and following up resumes involves a great deal of planning and skills that can be learned if you follow the many tips outlined in this chapter. Everything you have done thus far – assessing your interests and skills, developing an objective, and conducting research, and preparing for applications – should help you create a powerful and well-targeted resume.

TIP #70
Understand the critical role your resume plays in the whole job search process.

Many job seekers misunderstand the role of the resume. Some believe a resume will get them a job, and thus they try to put as much information on their resume as possible. However, the purpose of the resume is to get invited to a job interview. Like good advertising copy, it should be designed to persuade the reader to acquire the product, which in this case means inviting a candidate to a job interview. As

111

such, the resume needs to be carefully crafted with just enough information to grab readers' attention and persuade them to take action.

TIP #71
Write your own resume but seek assistance if necessary.

Whether or not you write your own resume depends on how good you are at writing and how much you are willing to spend on hiring a professional. Some people can do it on their own by following the advice and examples found in resume writing books. Others, however, have difficulty being very objective about themselves, putting all the elements together, and writing in the language of employers. After all, many of them were taught from childhood not to brag about themselves! While I prefer that you write your own resume because it will more accurately reflect your interests, skills, abilities, and goals, as I noted in Tip #13, I recognize that professional help is sometimes needed at critical stages of one's job search. If writing a resume is something you have difficulty doing, by all means seek professional help. Paying a professional to put together a winning resume will more than pay for itself if it results in job interviews and offers. A professional resume writer may charge from $100 to $600 to produce a first-class resume. If you are interested in contacting a professional resume writer, you are well advised to explore the resources on these professional resume writing and career websites:

> *Paying a professional resume writer $100 to $600 to craft a winning resume will more than pay for itself if it results in job interviews and offers.*

- Professional Association of Resume Writers and Career Coaches   www.parw.com

- Career Directors International www.careerdirectors.com

- National Resume Writers'
  Association   www.nrwaweb.com

- Career Management Alliance www.careermanagement
                                   alliance.com

Check out some of these websites which are sponsored by professional resume writers. Most of them will give you a free resume critique prior to using their fee-based services:

- A and A Resume   www.aandaresume.com
- A-Advanced Resume Service   www.topsecretresumes.com
- Advanced Career Systems   www.resumesystems.com
- Advanced Resume Services   www.resumeservices.com
- The Advantage   www.advantageresume.com
- Cambridge Resume Service   www.cambridgeresume.com
- Career Resumes   www.career-resumes.com
- CertifiedResumeWriters   http://certifiedresumewriters.
                                com
- eResumes (Rebecca Smith's) www.eresumes.com
- e-resume.net   www.e-resume.net
- myResumeAgent.com   www.myresumeagent.com
- Free-Resume-Tips   www.free-resume-tips.com
- ImpactResumes   www.impactresumes.com
- LeadingEdgeResumes   www.leadingedgeresumes.com
- ResumeAgent   www.resumeagent.com
- Resume.com   www.resume.com
- ResumeMaker   www.resumemaker.com
- ResumeWriter   www.resumewriter.com
- WSACORP.com   www.wsacorp.com

TIP #72
Spend sufficient time to craft a resume that represents the real you.

Writing a first-class resume that showcases your major strengths takes more than a few hours to complete. Assuming you have conducted a thorough self-assessment and crafted a targeted objective, developing each section of your resume will take some time. You'll want to draft and re-write each section, conduct both internal and external evaluations (see Tips #82 and #83), and write the final version for distribution. This whole process may take a few days or a couple of weeks. Whatever you do, make sure you spend sufficient time to complete each section of your resume. It needs to be perfect in every respect since it will represent your best effort to the reader. It could well lead to a terrific job that pays $30,000, $50,000, or $50,000+ more than you currently make.

TIP #73
Keep your resume to one or two pages.

Many individuals try to put their complete education and work history on their resumes which, in turn, translate into a very long document. The general rule of thumb for most job seekers is to write a one- or two-page resume. If you have fewer than 10 years of work experience, you may want to keep it to one page. If you have more than 10 years experience, a two-page resume would be appropriate. Unless you are an academic writing a curriculum vitae in lieu of a resume, which could run 10 to 30 pages, you should not exceed the two-page rule. The reasons for limiting the length of your resume are very simple. First, employers are very busy people who normally spend about 30 seconds reading a resume – a good reason to include lots of bulleted and highlighted items. In fact, they really don't read resumes in depth – only glance at them and focus on items that catch their attention. Nearly 70 percent of their attention is focused on the first page and 30 percent on the second page. If you go beyond two pages, chances are you will lose the reader's interest. Second, always remember that your resume, like good advertising copy, should immediately grab the attention of the reader and motivate him to contact you for an interview. If your resume is too long or too short, it will lack the power to persuade. If you have problems with this rule, keep in mind

> *Most executives making in excess of $300,000 a year write a two-page resume. If they can do it, so can you!*

that most executives making over $300,000 a year write two-page resumes. If they can get their qualifications on two pages, so can you!

You should write your resume based on a solid understanding of yourself as well as your audience. You do this by first analyzing yourself and your audience as you begin to link your aspirations to employers' needs. Remember, you are not writing the resume for your mother, spouse, yourself, or the newspaper obituary page.

TIP #74
Avoid common resume errors.

Many resumes are literally "dead upon arrival" because the job seeker made serious writing errors. Employers frequently report the following common mistakes resume writers make, which often eliminates them from competition. Most of these mistakes center on issues of focus, organization, trustworthiness, intelligence, and competence. Reading between the lines, employers often draw conclusions about the individual's personality and competence based upon the number of errors found on the resume. If you make any of these errors, chances are your **credibility** will be called into question. Make sure your resume does not commit any of these writing errors:

1. Unrelated to the position in question.
2. Too long or too short.
3. Unattractive with a poorly designed format, small type style, and crowded copy.
4. Misspellings, poor grammar, wordiness, and repetition.
5. Punctuation errors.
6. Lengthy phrases, long sentences, and awkward paragraphs.
7. Slick, amateurish, or "gimmicky" – appears over-produced.
8. Boastful, egocentric, and aggressive.
9. Dishonest, untrustworthy, or suspicious information.
10. Missing critical categories (i.e., experience and education)
11. Difficult to interpret because of poor organization and lack of focus – uncertain what the person has done or can do.
12. Unexplained time gaps between jobs.
13. Too many jobs in a short period of time – a job hopper with little evidence of career advancement.

14. No evidence of past accomplishments or a pattern of performance from which to predict future performance; primarily focuses on formal duties and responsibilities that came with previous jobs.

15. Lacks credibility and content – includes much fluff and "canned" resume language.

16. States a strange, unclear, or vague objective.

17. Appears over-qualified or under-qualified for the position.

18. Includes distracting personal information that does not enhance the resume nor candidacy.

19. Fails to include critical contact information, such as telephone number and email address, and uses an anonymous address (P.O. Box number).

20. Uses jargon and abbreviations unfamiliar to the reader.

21. Embellishes name with formal titles, middle names, and nicknames which make him or her appear odd or strange.

22. Repeatedly refers to "I" and appears self-centered.

23. Includes obvious self-serving references that raise credibility questions.

24. Sloppy, with handwritten corrections – crosses out "married" and writes "single"!

25. Includes "red flag" information such as being fired, lawsuits or claims, health or performance problems, or stating salary figures, including salary requirements, that may be too high or too low.

Assuming you have written a great resume and a very persuasive cover letter, your next challenge is to make sure you don't make several errors relating to the production, distribution, and follow-up stages of your resumes and letters. Here are some of the most common such errors you must avoid:

1. Poorly typed and reproduced – hard to read.
2. Produced on odd-sized paper.
3. Printed on poor quality paper or on extremely thin or thick paper.
4. Soiled with coffee stains, fingerprints, or ink marks.
5. Sent to the wrong person or department.

6. Mailed, faxed, or e-mailed to "To Whom It May Concern" or "Dear Sir."

7. Emailed as an attachment which could have a virus if opened.

8. Enclosed in a tiny envelope that requires the resume to be unfolded and flattened several times.

9. Arrived without proper postage – the employer gets to pay the extra!

10. Sent the resume and letter by the slowest postage rate possible.

11. Envelope double-sealed with tape and is indestructible – nearly impossible to open by conventional means!

12. Back of envelope includes a handwritten note stating that something is missing on the resume, such as a telephone number, email address, or new mailing address.

13. Resume taped to the inside of the envelope, an old European habit practiced by paranoid letter writers. Need to destroy the envelope and perhaps the resume as well to get it out.

14. Accompanied by extraneous or inappropriate enclosures which were not requested, such as copies of self-serving letters or recommendations, transcripts, or samples of work.

15. Arrives too late for consideration.

16. Comes without a cover letter.

17. Cover letter repeats what's on the resume – does not command attention nor move the reader to action.

18. Sent the same or different versions of the resume to the same person as a seemingly clever follow-up method.

19. Follow-up call made too soon – before the resume and letter arrive!

20. Follow-up call is too aggressive or the candidate appears too "hungry" for the position – appears needy or greedy.

Whatever you do, make sure you write, produce, and distribute error-free resumes and letters. If you commit any of the above errors, chances are you will be eliminated from consideration or your candidacy will be greatly diminished.

TIP #75
Include and exclude key information
categories on your resume.

The best structured chronological resumes include the following sequence of categories:

1. Contact Information
2. Objective
3. Summary of Qualifications
4. Professional Experience
5. Education
6. Professional Affiliations

Combination and functional resumes include other categories such as Work History. If you write a scannable resume, a Keyword Summary should replace the Objective and Summary of Qualifications.

You should avoid the following inappropriate categories that sometimes are included in resumes:

1. Sensitive personal information (age, height, weight, marital status, children, race, religion, political affiliation, disabilities, sexual orientation)
2. Previous salaries
3. Hobbies
4. Personal statements
5. References

Many of these items are inappropriate to raise at any time during your job search, and some are best left to a face-to-face interview. Knowing what to include or exclude on your resume may best be determined by the old rule *"When in doubt, throw it out!"*

TIP #76
Choose an appropriate resume format
and language.

There are many different types of resumes from which you can select an appropriate format to communicate your qualifications to employers. The most common types include:

1. **Chronological resume:** Everyone's favorite and the easiest to write since previous work experience is listed in reverse chronological order. Readers can easily see a pattern of work history as well as any employment gaps.

2. **Functional resume:** The least favorite resume for employers because it de-emphasizes employment dates, positions, and responsibilities. It's a favorite format for job seekers who lack work experience, have time gaps in their work history, or are changing careers. Beginning with a functional objective, functional resumes emphasize qualifications, functional skills, and related accomplishments. Often lacking substance, these resumes may raise more questions than they answer.

3. **Combination resumes:** This is a favorite resume for most job seekers who are able to combine the best elements of both combination and functional resumes. It allows you to stress your skills and competencies in functional terms while also providing the necessary work chronology.

4. **Resume letters:** This is a letter that substitutes for a resume. A more personal approach, it summarizes a candidate's employment goals and qualifications. When using this letter, your goal should be to communicate your skills and qualifications directly to a specific person in an organization.

All of these resumes should follow the same rules of good resume writing: be concise, use action verbs, identify the needs of the employer, talk about your accomplishments, and show how your abilities and skills can meet the employer's needs. For more information on how to develop these different types of resumes, including examples, see Ronald L. Krannich and William J. Banis, *High Impact Resumes and Letters* (Impact Publications). It's included in the order form at the end of this book.

TIP #77
Emphasize your skills and accomplishments throughout your resume.

Most job seekers make the mistake of explaining previous employment in terms of formal duties and responsibilities. While such language may impress the resume writer because it indicates a position's level of responsibility, it is less impressive to resume readers who know that duties and responsibilities come with a position regardless of who performs in the position. To what degree you performed those duties and responsibilities and with what outcomes for the employer are different issues altogether. If you frame your experience in terms of achievements or accomplishments – specific and quantifiable outcomes – you give the reader a sense of your pattern of performance or what I earlier (Tip #39) called your Motivated Abilities and Skills (MAS).

TIP #78
Be honest but not stupid on your resume.

The truth can be told many different ways. If you have red flags in your background – incarcerated, fired, job hopper, expelled from school, lack skills – there is no reason for you to include such information on your resume. These are issues that may come up in job interviews. Why would you want to prematurely eliminate yourself from consideration for a job interview by revealing your good, bad, and ugly sides on your resume? Here are a few examples of being stupid on different sections of a resume:

Objective: Get some work experience so I'll have a better idea what I want to do in the future.

Experience: Reason for leaving this position: fired.

2004-2007. Served time for burglary in Medina State Penitentiary.

Education: Did not complete my degree because I was expelled from college for drug use.

While all of these statements may be truthful and the candidate may be complimented for his frankness, they are all stupid and inappropriate statements to include on a resume. Again, what's the purpose of a resume? To get a job interview, period. Watch carefully how you tell the truth. Sins of omission are always preferable to sins of commission when writing a resume. A job search is not the place to voluntarily confess your sins. Use common sense and be tactful when writing each section of your resume.

> *Sins of omission are always preferable to sins of commission when writing a resume.*

TIP #79
Produce both a paper and electronic resume.

Since more and more employers want you to email your resume, which can be scanned into a resume database, you are well advised to complete both a traditional paper resume and an electronic resume. Electronic resumes follow different rules, such as using keywords and electronic formatting. In fact, in today's job market you will encounter several different types of electronic resumes that are more or less accepted by employers, depending on their particular requirements:

1. ASCII or plain-text resumes
2. Formatted resumes
3. PDF resumes
4. HTML or web page resumes
5. Online portfolios
6. Posted resumes

For more information on electronic resumes and online portfolios, see Joyce Lain Kennedy's *Resumes for Dummies* (John Wiley), Susan Whitcomb's and Pat Kendall's *e-Resumes* (McGraw-Hill), Pat Criscito's *e-Resumes* (Barron's Educational), and Susan Amirian's and Eleanor Flanigan's, *Create Your Digital Portfolio* (JIST Publishing). See the order form at the end of this book.

TIP #80
Prepare to mail, fax, and email your resume.

Since more and more employers want candidates to email them their resume, you need to be prepared for sending a first-rate emailed resume. Do not send your resume as an attachment, unless an employer asks you to do so. Because attachments these days are often accompanied by viruses, many people routinely delete email messages sent to them by strangers. If you send an ASCII, plain-text, or PDF resume, make sure you know what it looks like at the recipient's end by either emailing it to yourself or to a friend first.

> *Do not send your resume as an attachment, unless an employer asks you to do so.*

While many employers still ask for mailed and faxed resumes, today fewer and fewer do so. If you fax your resume, be sure to include a cover sheet as well as a cover letter. Mailed resumes are best sent flat in a 9 x 12" envelope.

TIP #81
Project a professional image with
a first-class resume.

The very first thing an employer encounters from a candidate is his or her resume. Make sure your resume has the look and feel of quality. If you are sending a traditional paper resume, observe all the rules on size (8½ x 11"), color (conservative white, ivory, or light gray), and quality of the paper (20 to 50 lb. bond with 100 percent cotton fiber) and production (laser-quality printer).

TIP #82
Conduct an internal evaluation
of your resume.

An internal resume evaluation identifies the strengths and weaknesses of your resume in reference to numerous principles of effective resume writing. Take the questionnaire below, and be sure to follow each weak rating with a note to yourself on improving your resume. This activity enables you to evaluate **and** follow through in revising the resume. Refer to the following evaluation criteria to conduct your internal evaluation.

INSTRUCTIONS: Examine your resume writing skills in reference to the following evaluation criteria. Respond to each statement by circling the appropriate number to the right that most accurately describes your resume:

1 = Strongly agree   4 = Disagree
2 = Agree   5 = Strongly disagree
3 = So-so (neutral)

1. Wrote the resume myself – no creative
   plagiarizing from others' resume examples.   1   2   3   4   5

2. Conducted a thorough self-assessment which
   became the basis for writing each resume
   section.   1   2   3   4   5

3. Have a plan of action that relates my resume
   to other job search activities.   1   2   3   4   5

4. Selected an appropriate resume format that
   best presents my interests, skills, and
   experience.   1   2   3   4   5

5. Included all essential information
   categories in the proper order.   1   2   3   4   5

6. Eliminated all extraneous information
   unrelated to my objective and employers'
   needs (date, picture, race, religion, political
   affiliation, age, sex, height, weight, marital
   status, health, hobbies) or better saved for
   discussion in the interview (salary history
   and references).   1   2   3   4   5

7. Put the most important information first.   1   2   3   4   5

8. Resume is oriented to the future rather
   than to the past.   1   2   3   4   5

9. Contact information is complete – name, address, phone and fax numbers, email. No P.O. Box numbers or nicknames.   1   2   3   4   5

10. Limited abbreviations to accepted words.   1   2   3   4   5

11. Contact information attractively formatted to introduce the resume.   1   2   3   4   5

12. Included a thoughtful employer-oriented objective that incorporates both skills and benefits/outcomes.   1   2   3   4   5

13. Objective clearly communicates to employers what I want to do, can do, and will do for them.   1   2   3   4   5

14. Objective is neither too general nor too specific.   1   2   3   4   5

15. Objective serves as the central organizing element for all other sections of the resume.   1   2   3   4   5

16. Included a powerful "Summary of Qualifications" or "Professional Profile" section immediately following the "Objective."   1   2   3   4   5

17. Elaborated work experience in detail, emphasizing my skills, abilities, and achievements.   1   2   3   4   5

18. Each "Experience" section is short and to the point.   1   2   3   4   5

19. Consistently used action verbs and active voice.   1   2   3   4   5

20. Did not refer to myself as "I."   1   2   3   4   5

21. Used specifics – numbers and percentages – to highlight my performance.   1   2   3   4   5

22. Included positive quotations about my performance from previous employers.   1   2   3   4   5

23. Eliminated any negative references,
    including reasons for leaving.   1   2   3   4   5

24. Does not include names of supervisors or
    others involved with my professional or
    personal life.   1   2   3   4   5

25. Summarized my most recent job and then
    included other jobs in reverse chronological
    order.   1   2   3   4   5

26. Descriptions of "Experience" are consistent.   1   2   3   4   5

27. Put the most important skills information
    first when summarizing "Experience."   1   2   3   4   5

28. No time gaps nor "job hopping" apparent
    to reader.   1   2   3   4   5

29. Documented "other experience" that might
    strengthen my objective and decided to
    either include or exclude it on the resume.   1   2   3   4   5

30. Included complete information on my
    educational background, including
    important highlights.   1   2   3   4   5

31. If a recent graduate with little relevant
    work experience, emphasized educational
    background more than work experience.   1   2   3   4   5

32. Put education in reverse chronological
    order and eliminated high school if a
    college graduate.   1   2   3   4   5

33. Included special education and training
    relevant to my major interests and skills.   1   2   3   4   5

34. Included professional affiliations and
    membership relevant to my objective and
    skills; highlighted any major contributions.   1   2   3   4   5

35. Documented any special skills not included
    elsewhere on resume and included those
    that appear relevant to employers' needs.   1   2   3   4   5

36. Included awards or special recognition that further document my skills and achievements.   1   2   3   4   5

37. Weighed pros and cons of including a personal statement on my resume.   1   2   3   4   5

38. Did not mention salary history or expectations.   1   2   3   4   5

39. Did not include names, addresses, and phone numbers of references.   1   2   3   4   5

40. Included additional information to enhance the interest of employers.   1   2   3   4   5

41. Used a language appropriate for the employer, including terms that associate me with the industry.   1   2   3   4   5

42. My language is crisp, succinct, expressive, and direct.   1   2   3   4   5

43. Used highlighting and emphasizing techniques to make the resume most readable.   1   2   3   4   5

44. Resume has an inviting, uncluttered look, incorporating sufficient white space and using a standard type style and size.   1   2   3   4   5

45. Kept the design basic and conservative.   1   2   3   4   5

46. Kept sentences short and succinct.   1   2   3   4   5

47. Resume runs one or two pages.   1   2   3   4   5

TOTAL

Add the numbers you circled to the right of each statement to get a cumulative score. If your score is higher than 85, you need to work on improving various aspects of your resume.

TIP #83
Subject your resume to an external evaluation.

You should conduct an **external resume evaluation** by circulating your resume to three or more individuals. For guidelines, give your evaluators the form on page 128. But most important of all, choose people whose opinions are objective, frank, and thoughtful. Do not select friends and relatives who usually flatter you with positive comments. Professional acquaintances or people you don't know personally but whom you admire may be good evaluators. An ideal evaluator has experience in hiring

> *The ideal evaluator has experience in hiring people in your area of job interest.*

people in your area of job interest. In addition to sharing their experience with you, they may refer you to other individuals who would be interested in your qualifications. If you choose such individuals to critique your resume, ask them for their frank reaction – not what they would politely say to a candidate presenting such a resume. You want the people to role play with you – a potential interview candidate. Ask your evaluators:

"If you don't mind, would you look over my resume? Perhaps you could comment on its clarity or make suggestions for improving it?"

"How would you react to this resume if you received it from a candidate? Would it grab your attention and interest you enough to invite the person to an interview?"

"If you were writing this resume, what changes would you make? Any additions, deletions, modifications?"

External Evaluation

INSTRUCTIONS: Circle the number that best characterizes various aspects of my resume. Please include any recommendations on how I could best improve the resume:

1 = Excellent   2 = Okay   3 = Weak

Recommendations for Improvement

1. Overall appearance	1	2	3
2. Layout	1	2	3
3. Clarity	1	2	3
4. Consistency	1	2	3
5. Readability	1	2	3
6. Language	1	2	3
7. Organization	1	2	3
8. Content/completeness	1	2	3
9. Length	1	2	3
10. Contact information/ header	1	2	3
11. Objective	1	2	3
12. Experience	1	2	3
13. Skills	1	2	3
14. Achievements	1	2	3
15. Education	1	2	3
16. Other information	1	2	3

Such an evaluation should especially take place in the process of networking and conducting informational interviews (Chapter 9).

You will normally receive good cooperation and advice by approaching people in this manner. In addition, you will probably get valuable unsolicited advice on other job search matters, such as job leads, job market information, and employment strategies.

In contrast to the closed and deductive nature of the internal evaluation, the external evaluation should be open-ended and inductive. Avoid preconceived evaluation categories; let the evaluator react to you and your resume as if you were in a job interview situation.

Taken together, the internal and external evaluations should complement each other by providing you with maximum information for revising your draft resume.

TIP #84
Send your resume to a real person.

Always try to get a name of a person to whom you should address your resume. Depending on the position and how it is being screened, in some cases the person will be in the human resources or personnel department. In other cases it will be the hiring manager. Addressing your resume "To Whom It May Concern" or "Human Resources" is a good way to lose your resume. When it comes time to follow up on your resume, you will have no one to contact to discuss your candidacy. If you don't have a name, call the organization and company and ask for a name to whom you should address your resume. Always address the person by his or her last name – Mr. _____, Mrs. _____, or Ms. _____. If the company will not give you a name, try to at least get a position so you have some idea at what level your resume will be reviewed.

TIP #85
Post your resume to various employment websites.

Over 25,000 websites in the United States deal with employment. Yes, there's a jungle on the Internet as many job seekers face a daunting task of deciding which sites to visit and possibly use. A good starting point for making such decisions is Dick Bolles's gateway site to today's most popular job boards:

www.jobhuntersbible.com/jobsresumes/sec_page.php?sub_item=054

Also, we sure to check out the latest speculation concerning the future demise of traditional job boards in the face of social networking sites that are playing an increasing role in what is called Web 2.0 social networking sites and second generation job boards:

www.quintcareers.com/QC_job-board-death_news-release.html

For now, you'll probably want to concentrate on several of the most popular employment websites:

- Monster.com — www.monster.com
- JobCentral — www.jobcentral.com
- Emurse.com — www.emurse.com
- America's Job Bank — www.jobbankinfo.org
- CareerBuilder — www.careerbuilder.com
- NationJob — www.nationjob.com
- FlipDog — http://flipdog.com
- Hot Jobs Yahoo — http://hotjobs.yahoo.com
- Jobs.com — www.jobs.com
- JobSearch — http://jobsearch.monster.com
- CareerJournal — www.careerjournal.com
- CareerFlex — www.careerflex.com
- Employment911.com — www.employment911.com
- EmploymentSpot — www.employmentspot.com
- WorkTree — www.worktree.com
- JobSniper — www.jobsniper.com
- Vault.com — www.vault.com
- WetFeet.com — www.wetfeet.com
- PlanetRecruit — www.planetrecruit.com
- BestJobsUSA — www.bestjobsusa.com
- MRINetwork.com — www.mrinetwork.com
- CareerShop — www.careershop.com
- MonsterTrak.com — www.monstertrak.monster.com

- Kenexa	www.kenexa.com
- Career.com	www.career.com
- JobBank USA	www.jobbankusa.com
- Net-Temps	www.net-temps.com
- Emplymentwizard.com	www.emplymentwizard.com
- American Preferred Jobs	www.preferredjobs.com
- ProHire	www.prohire.com
- Careerxchange	www.careerxchange.com
- Career Magazine	www.careermag.com
- Employers Online	www.employersonline.com
- EmployMax	www.employmax.com
- EmploymentGuide	www.employmentguide.com
- Wanted Technologies	www.wantedtech.com
- Arbita	www.arbita.net
- Recruiters Online Network	www.recruitersonline.com
- kForce.com	www.kforce.com
- Dice.com	www.dice.com
- Washington Post	www.washingtonpost.com/ wl/jobs

While you should visit the large employment websites, don't put much hope in their ability to locate a job or employer for you. Large employment websites such as Monster.com, HotJobs.Yahoo.com, and Career Builder.com offer a wealth of information and services to both employers and job seekers. However, these sites are primarily run for the benefit of the paying customers – employers. Job seekers can post their resumes online, browse job postings, and apply for jobs through these sites, but few ever get jobs through these sites. The most valuable aspects of these sites for job seekers are the peripheral services which are designed to keep you coming back again and again (in this online business, you're known as "traffic" when sites set their advertising rates for employers):

- Job Search Tips
- Featured Articles
- Career Experts or Advisors
- Career Tool Kit
- Career Assessment Tests
- Community Forums
- Discussion or Chat Groups
- Message Boards
- Job Alert ("Push") Emails
- Company Research Centers
- Networking Forums
- Salary Calculators/Wizards

- Resume Management Center
- Resume and Cover Letter Advice
- Multimedia Resume Software
- Job Interview Practice
- Relocation Information
- Reference Check Checkers
- Employment or Career News
- Free Email for Privacy
- Success Stories
- Career Newsletter
- Career Events
- Online Job Fairs
- Affiliate Sites
- Career Resources
- Featured Employers
- Polls and Surveys
- Contests
- Online Education and Training
- International Employment
- Talent Auction Centers
- Company Ads (buttons and banners)
- Sponsored Links
- Special Channels for students, executives, freelancers, military, and others

Huge mega employment sites such as <u>Monster.com</u> include over 80 percent of these add-on services. That site alone is well worth visiting again and again for tips and advice. Most sites, however, only include job postings and resume databases and maybe a newsletter designed to capture email addresses of job seekers who must register in order to receive the newsletter. Again, don't expect too much from these sites in terms of connecting with employers who will invite you to interviews. They have hundreds of thousands of resumes in their databases. Your chances of getting a job interview based on your presence in such databases is not very good. However, you may get lucky given your particular mix of skills and experience. My advice is to post your resume on many such websites and see what happens. Make sure your resume includes lots of keywords descriptive of your skills and accomplishments, since employers will scan the resume databases based upon keyword search.

You are well advised to focus on smaller specialty websites relevant to your occupation and industry. Many users of Internet employment websites focus most of their attention on a few huge employment sites, such as <u>Monster.com</u> and <u>HotJobs.Yahoo.com</u>. However, they would be better using employment websites that specialize in their industry. For example, if you are an IT professional, your chances of connecting with an employer are much greater on <u>Dice.com</u> and <u>ItCareers.com</u>

than on the top 10 mega employment sites. Employers interested in hiring IT professionals are more likely to use these specialty sites than the more general mega employment sites.

Using the Internet in your job search is relatively easy once you have some basic guidance on where to go and what to do. The following books provide details on using the Internet for finding a job. Several of these resources go through the whole process of using the Internet for conducting employment research, posting resumes, and communicating by email. Others primarily annotate the best sites on the Internet:

> *You are well advised to focus on smaller specialty websites relevant to your occupation and industry.*

100 Top Internet Job Sites (Kristina M. Ackley)
America's Top Internet Job Sites (Ron and Caryl Krannich)
Career Exploration on the Internet (Ferguson Publishing)
The Directory of Websites for International Jobs (Ron and Caryl Krannich)
The Everything Online Job Search Book (Steve Graber)
The Guide to Internet Job Searching (Margaret Riley Dikel)
Haldane's Best Employment Websites for Professionals (Bernard Haldane Associates)
Job-Hunting Online (Mark Emery Bolles and Richard Nelson Bolles)
Weddle's Job-Seeker's Guide to Employment Web Sites (Peter D. Weddle)

Also, be sure to examine these Internet resources on writing electronic and Internet resumes:

Electronic Resumes and Online Networking (Rebecca Smith)
e-Resumes (Susan Britton Whitcomb and Pat Kendall)
e-Resumes (Pat Criscito)
Internet Resumes (Peter D. Weddle)
Resumes for Dummies (Joyce Lain Kennedy)

TIP #86
Avoid broadcasting your resume to hundreds of potential employers.

It's always best to target your resume to specific employers whom you know are hiring for specific positions related to your qualifications. The broadcast method gives you a false sense of making progress in the job market because you are sending out lots of resumes and letters to lots of employers. You'll be lucky to get a 1-percent response rate from such junk mailings. However, if you are in a high-demand field, such as chemical engineering, have unique or exotic skills, demonstrate lots of experience, and make more than $100,000 a year, the broadcast letter may work better for you. You might want to broadcast your resume to two audiences – headhunters and employers.

> *The broadcast method gives you a false sense of making progress in the job market.*

If and when you decide to play this game – knowing full well the odds are probably against you – start by investigating several fee-based resume distribution firms (your cyberspace "blasters"). Try to find out the relative mix in their database of recruiters versus actual employers who might be looking for someone with your qualifications. These sites know the "mix" since they require employers and recruiters to sign up or register to receive "free" resumes from these services. For example, one of the largest such firms, www.resumezapper.com, tells you up front that they only work with third party recruiters and search firms – no employers; they primarily appeal to candidates who prefer being marketed through an executive recruiter. The recipients of these free resumes usually specify filters, so they only receive resumes that meet their marketing criteria. Not surprisingly, most of these resume distribution sites will blast your resume almost solely to recruiters or headhunters. Some sites, such as www.resumeagent.com and www.resumerabbit.com, will blast your resume to numerous sites that have resume databases, thus saving time in entering your resume into each unique resume database.

- Allen and Associates www.resumexpress.com
- CareerXpress.com www.careerxpress.com
- E-cv.com www.e-cv.com
- myResumeAgent.com www.myresumeagent.com
- HotResumes www.hotresumes.com
- Job Search Page www.jobsearchpage.com
  (international focus)
- Job Village www.jobvillage.com
- Resume Agent www.resumeagent.com
- ResumeBlaster www.resumeblaster.com
- Resume Booster www.resumebooster.com
- ResumeMachine.com www.resumemachine.com
- Resume Rabbit www.resumerabbit.com
- ResumeZapper www.resumezapper.com
- RocketResume www.rocketresume.com
- See Me Resumes www.seemeresumes.com
- WSACORP.com www.wsacorp.com

If you want to try your luck, for anywhere from $19.95 to over $4,000, these resume blasting firms will send your resume to 1,000 to 10,000 headhunters and employers who seek such resumes. While I do not endorse these firms – and I am often skeptical about what appear to be inflated claims of effectiveness – nonetheless, you may want to explore a few of these firms. Good luck!

TIP #87
If appropriate, send your resume to executive recruiters and CEOs.

If you expect to be making $100,000+ a year, chances are you will find over 90 percent of the Internet employment sites irrelevant to your job search. You have very special employment needs that are best met by connecting with headhunters and CEOs rather than surveying job listings and entering your resume in a mega resume database that is primarily accessed by human resources personnel for lower level positions. As noted in Tip #86, several resume blasting services focus on getting resumes in the hands of such employment brokers. At the same time, a few websites focus on executive-level candidates. They offer databases and networking opportunities that both include and bypass executive recruiters. You should start with the following gateway site to executive recruiters:

www.i-recruit.com

Individuals interested in executive-level positions are well advised to visit the following sites. Several of them charge a monthly or quarterly "membership" fee to access their site while others are free. I recommend starting with the free sites since they may prove to be just as effective as the fee-based sites (I've seen no evidence to the contrary, but you'll have to be the judge). The free sites include:

- **6 Figure Jobs**   www.sixfigurejobs.com
- **Monster.com**   www.monster.com
- **Management Recruiters International**   www.mrinetwork.com
- **Recruiters Online Network**   www.recruitersonline.com

Major fee-based sites for executive-level job seekers include:

- **ExecuNet**   www.execunet.com
- **ExecutivesOnly**   www.executivesonly.com
- **Netshare**   www.netshare.com

TIP #88
Develop a good record keeping system for following up your resume.

As you begin applying for many positions and networking for informational interviews, you will need to rely on something more than your memory. A good record-keeping system can help you manage your job search effectively, especially the numerous resumes and letters you have sent. You can do this the old fashioned way by purchasing file folders for your correspondence and notes. Be sure to make copies of all letters you write since you may need to refer to them over the telephone or before interviews. Record your activities with each employer – letters, resumes, telephone calls, interviews – on a 4" x 6" card and file it according to the name of the organization or individual. These files will help you quickly access information and evaluate your job search progress.

If you're computer savvy, you may want to electronically organize your recordkeeping activities using database and contact management programs, such as **_ACT!_** and **_Outlook_**. Check your current software programs for a contact manager, calendar, or tracking/follow-up program. Several software programs are now available for networking and tracking activities. Some, such as **_WinWay Resume_**, **_ResumeMaker_**, **_JobTabs_**, **_JibberJobber_**, **_Sharkware_**, and **_Job Hunt Express_**, are designed specifically for tracking job leads and following up specific job search activities. Many of the large employment websites, such as Monster.com, allow you to manage your resume and track applications online.

One of the simplest and most effective paper and pencil systems consists of recording data on 4" x 6" cards. If you respond to classified ads, clip the ad and paste it to the card. Label the card in the upper left-hand corner with a useful reference category and subcategory. For example, in applying for a management trainee position with a food company, your category might appear as follows: MANAGEMENT TRAINEE – food. In the upper right-hand corner, place the name of the company. At the bottom of the card identify the name, title, address, and phone number, and email of your contact. On the reverse side of the same card, record all information pertinent to making contacts for this position. Organize this information by dates and the nature of the contact. Add any information which documents your continuing contacts.

TIP #89
Quickly follow up each resume with a telephone call or email.

Once you send resumes to prospective employers, be sure to follow up within five days after they receive your resume. If the employer has received many resumes during this time period, your telephone call or email will remind him or her who you are and your interest in the position. I prefer using the phone for doing this follow-up. A phone call also may give the employer an opportunity to conduct a telephone screening interview – something that may give you an advantage over the competition!

Don't be too pushy at this stage. Use a low-key professional approach. Assuming you are able to get through to the person who received your resume (see Tip #84 on the importance of addressing your resume to a name), ask about your resume and the position:

> Hi, this is Emily Orlando. I'm calling in reference to my resume which I sent to you on June 3rd.
>
> Did you receive it?
>
> I know you're busy, but did you have a chance to review it yet?
>
> Do you have any questions at time?
>
> As I mentioned in my cover letter, I'm very much interested in this position, especially given my recent work at Rogers and Associates which focused on developing a new financial planning program for college graduates. I would love to have an opportunity to meet with you to discuss my work and how my experience might best contribute to your new programs designed for college students. Could we meet soon?

Notice how this conversation line moves from a polite *"Did you receive my resume?"* question to stressing the individual's key strength in reference to the employer's hiring need. Most important of all, this individual closes this follow-up call with an action statement – a request to interview for the job. While this is a moderately assertive approach, it is very targeted and professional. Although the employer may not wish to interview this individual right now, he or she may remember the candidate, re-read her resume, and put her at the top of the interview list. Being **remembered and prioritized** are two of the most desirable outcomes of such a resume follow-up call.

For insider tips on how to best use the telephone in your job search, with special emphasis on highly effective voicemail techniques, see Neil P. McNulty's and Ronald L. Krannich's *The Quick 30/30 Job Solution: Smart Job Search Tips for Surviving Today's New Economy* (Impact Publications).

8

Cover and Job Search Letter Tips

COVER LETTERS AND OTHER types of job search letters are often more important to getting a job interview and offer than a resume. Indeed, many employers report it was the cover or thank-you letter that made the difference in selecting candidates. In fact, many job seekers have been hired on the basis of their letter writing skills rather than their resume.

Don't under-estimate the power of a letter. Too many job seekers primarily focus on the content of their resume to the exclusion of letters. Some of them treat letters as a necessary nuisance and thus produce canned or uninspired letters that diminish their candidacy. Don't let this happen to you. Be sure to pay particular attention to a whole series of letters that need to be written at various stages of your job search. These letters can make a big difference between being accepted or rejected for a job interview and offer.

The following tips introduce you to some of the most important written job search communication. If you follow these tips, you should be able to energize your job search as you express your unique personality and values to employers.

TIP #90
Your resume always should be accompanied by a cover letter.

If you want your resume to be "dead upon arrival," just send it without a cover letter or write a short note at the top of your resume, such as *"Please consider me for a position with your company."* Here's the problem: if you are too lazy to craft a thoughtful cover letter, you're also too thoughtless to be considered for a job. Cover letters are an important part of job search etiquette. Employers expect to receive them. They want candidates to communicate information

> *If you are too lazy to craft a thoughtful cover letter, you're also too thoughtless to be considered for a job.*

about themselves that is not included in the resume, such as their personality, enthusiasm, and competence. If you view your cover letter as being potentially more important than your resume in getting a job interview, you just might spend a great deal of time crafting a very thoughtful and powerful cover letter.

TIP #91
Carefully craft and proofread every word, sentence, and paragraph.

Like the resume, your letters should be picture perfect – no misspellings or grammatical errors. Be sure to proofread your letters very carefully. Also, have someone else read your letters for errors and content.

TIP #92
Avoid repeating the content of your resume in a cover letter.

Too many job seekers merely repeat the content of their resume in the cover letter. A cover letter should include unique content – things that are not included in the resume. Most important of all, the cover letter should be designed to persuade the reader to take action, which means inviting you to the interview. You might, for example, open with an attention-grabbing question or statement, such as *"Are you looking for someone who can increase sales by 30 percent a year? I have done so for the past five years as . . . "* Wherever you do, avoid such standard openers as *"Please find enclosed a copy of my resume in response to your . . . "* This is a dull and formal opener that may stop the reader at the end of the first sentence. It doesn't separate you from the competition. It does little to express your enthusiasm, energy, and personality. It's simply deadly and thus may kill your resume!

> *Your cover letter should be designed to persuade the reader to take action – invite you to the interview.*

TIP #93
Write a variety of job search letters appropriate for different job search situations.

Cover letters, which accompany resumes, are only one of several types of letters you need to write during your job search. Other important job search letters include:

- Resume letters
- Approach letters
- Thank-you letters

Some of the most powerful job search letters you can write are thank-you letters. These letters are usually remembered by employers because few candidates are thoughtful enough to send such letters. Different types of thank-you letters should be written on various job search occasions:

- Post-job interview
- After an informational interview

- Responding to a rejection
- Withdrawing from consideration
- Accepting a job offer
- Terminating employment

These are some of the most neglected yet most important written communications in any job search. If you write these letters, your job search may take you much further than you expected. Indeed, you may be surprised by the positive responses to your candidacy! Numerous examples of these types of job search letters can be found in Ron and Caryl Krannich's *201 Dynamite Job Search Letters* and Wendy S. Enelow's *Best Cover Letters for $100,000+ Jobs* (Impact Publications). See the order form at the end of this book.

TIP #94
Avoid using canned language in your letters.

Employers normally receive the same types of uninspired job search letters – job seekers tend to use canned language that appears to be taken from a book on letter writing. Few such letters grab the attention of readers and persuade them to respond positively to the writer. Such cover letter phrases as *"Please find enclosed . . . ," "I'm pleased to learn about . . . ," "As summarized in the enclosed resume . . . ," "I appreciate your consideration," "I look forward to*

> *Let the employer know you are different from the competition and that you really want the job.*

hearing from you,"* and *"Please give me a call if you have any questions"* are good examples of canned and uninspired language. Make sure your letters avoid such language as you focus on expressing your unique personality, energy, and enthusiasm. Be different and bold – write a letter that truly expresses who you are in terms of interests, skills, and goals; orient it toward taking action. Let the employer know you are different from the competition and that you really want the job.

TIP #95
Use positive and performance-oriented language throughout your letters.

Similar to the choice of language throughout your job search (Tip #29) and on your resume (Tip #77), you want to impress upon the employer that you are a performer who has a pattern of performance – someone who regularly achieves results. In so doing, you need to provide examples, stories, and statistics of your achievements. Avoid any negative language that could be misinterpreted as a potential red flag.

TIP #96
Structure your cover letter for action.

Keep your cover letter short and to the point. Three paragraphs should suffice:

1. State your interest and purpose. Try to link your interests to the employer's needs.

2. Highlight your enclosed resume by stressing what you will do for the employer in reference to the employer's specific needs.

3. Request an interview and indicate you will soon call to schedule an appointment.

Page 144 includes a good example of such a letter written in response to a specific job vacancy. It is purposeful without being overly aggressive or boastful. The writer's purpose is already known by the employer. The first paragraph should re-state the position listed as well as the source of information. It links the writer's interests to the employer's needs. The writer also indicates knowledge of the organization. Overall, the first paragraph is succinct, purposeful, and thoughtful. The writer invites the reader to learn more about him.

931 Davis Street
Boston, MA 01931
January 18, _____

John F. Baird, Manager
Hopkins International Corporation
7532 Grand Avenue
Boston, MA 01937

Dear Mr. Baird:

Your listing in the January 17 issue of the <u>Daily News</u> for a managerial trainee interests me for several reasons. I possess the necessary experience and skills you outline in the ad. Your company has a fine reputation for quality products and a track record of innovation and growth. I seek a challenging position which will fully use my talents.

My experience and skills are summarized in the enclosed resume. You may be interested in several additional qualifications I would bring to this position:

- the ability to relate well to others
- a record of accomplishments and a desire to achieve better results
- a willingness to take on new responsibilities
- enthusiasm and initiative

I would appreciate more information concerning this position as well as an opportunity to meet with you to discuss our mutual interests. I will call you Thursday morning concerning any questions we both may have and to arrange an interview if we deem it is appropriate at that time.

I appreciate your consideration and look forward to meeting you.

Sincerely yours,

Steven Reeves

Steven Reeves

In the second paragraph the writer generates additional interest by referring to his enclosed resume and including additional information for emphasizing his qualifications vis-a-vis the employer's needs. The writer also attempts to re-write the employer's ad around his qualifications. In so doing, this writer should stand out from other candidates, because he **raises** the expectations of the employer beyond the position description. The writer, in effect, suggests to the employer that they will be getting more for their money than anticipated. This paragraph does not appear hyped, boastful, or aggressive. It is low-keyed yet assertive.

> *Let the employer know you are different from the competition and that you really want the job.*

In the third paragraph of this example, the writer makes an open-ended offer to the employer which is difficult to refuse. Linking his interest to the reader's, the writer softens the interview request without putting the employer on the spot of having to say "yes" or "no." Overall, the writer presents the employer with an opportunity to examine his **value**. Accompanied by an outstanding resume, this letter should make a positive impression on the employer. A phone call within 48 hours of receiving the letter will further enhance the writer's candidacy.

TIP #97
Make your letters unique by expressing your personality, energy, and enthusiasm.

Resumes follow a standard screening format that emphasizes descriptive information organized into standard resume categories. The main focus of resumes is on providing details on a candidate's goals, education, and work history. Except for the crisp and succinct language for detailing such information, resumes say little about the personality and behavior of individuals. On the other hand, job search letters provide candidates with opportunities to express their unique personality, energy, and enthusiasm – key values and qualities sought by many employers. Be sure to craft a unique letter that expresses such qualities to prospective employers.

TIP #98
Include a follow-up/action statement indicating what you intend to do next.

A letter without an action statement is a relatively ineffective job search letter. Without being overly aggressive, you can suggest an appropriate time for discussing your candidacy. This is usually done in the closing paragraph of an approach or cover letter. An effective statement goes something like this: *"I'll call you on Thursday afternoon to see if you have any questions."* This statement should command the attention of the reader who, in turn, takes notice of the fact that you will be calling at a specific time. If and when you include such follow-up statements, be sure you actually follow up. If not, such a statement becomes ineffective.

9

Networking and Informational Interviewing Tips

ETWORKING SHOULD PLAY a major role in landing interviews and job offers. The key dynamic for uncovering the hidden job market (Tip #7), networking plugs you into the word-of-mouth employment world where you learn about job openings **before** they are advertised. Since nearly 75 percent of all jobs are never advertised, you need to develop a strategy for uncovering jobs on the hidden job market. A well developed networking strategy based upon tips outlined in this chapter will put you in the right places at the right time to uncover some of the best jobs available and develop useful contacts for landing a job.

TIP #99
Test your networking I.Q.

Just how savvy a networker are you when it comes to connecting to influential people, finding a job, and advancing your career? Do you have the necessary networking skills for success, which include the ability to connect, build, and nurture networks of important relationships? Can you quickly network your way to job and career success, or do you need to focus on developing specific networking skills? Let's identify "Your Savvy Networking I.Q." You can quickly do this by responding to the following set of agree/disagree statements that relate to your networking skills:

Your Savvy Networking I.Q.

INSTRUCTIONS: Respond to each statement by circling the number to the right that best represents your situation. The higher your score, the higher your "Savvy Networking IQ."

SCALE: 5 = Strongly agree   2 = Disagree
            4 = Agree   1 = Strongly disagree
            3 = Maybe, not certain

1. I enjoy going to business and social
   functions where I have an opportunity to
   meet new people. (CONNECT/BUILD)   5 4 3 2 1

2. I usually take the initiative in introducing
   myself to people I don't know. (CONNECT)   5 4 3 2 1

3. I enjoy being in groups and actively
   participating in group activities.
   (CONNECT/BUILD)   5 4 3 2 1

4. On a scale of 1 to 10, my social skills
   are at least a "9." (BUILD/NURTURE)   5 4 3 2 1

5. I listen carefully and give positive
   feedback when someone is speaking
   to me. (CONNECT/BUILD)   5 4 3 2 1

6. I have a friendly and engaging
   personality that attracts others to me.
   (CONNECT/BUILD/NURTURE)   5 4 3 2 1

7. I make a special effort to remember
   people's names and frequently address
   them by their name. (CONNECT)   5 4 3 2 1

8. I carry business cards and often give
   them to acquaintances from whom I
   also collect business cards. (CONNECT)   5 4 3 2 1

9. I have a system for organizing business
   cards I receive, including notes on the
   back of each card. (BUILD)   5 4 3 2 1

10. I seldom have a problem starting a conversation and engaging in small talk with strangers. (CONNECT)   5 4 3 2 1

11. I enjoy making cold calls and persuading strangers to meet with me. (CONNECT)   5 4 3 2 1

12. I usually return phone calls in a timely manner. (CONNECT)   5 4 3 2 1

13. If I can't get through to someone on the phone, I'll keep trying until I do, even if it means making 10 more calls. (CONNECT)   5 4 3 2 1

14. I follow up on new contacts by phone, email, or letter. (BUILD)   5 4 3 2 1

15. I have several friends who will give me job leads. (BUILD)   5 4 3 2 1

16. I frequently give and receive referrals. (BUILD)   5 4 3 2 1

17. I have many friends. (BUILD)   5 4 3 2 1

18. I engage in online social networking through such sites as MySpace, Facebook, and LinkedIn. (CONNECT/BUILD)   5 4 3 2 1

19. I know at least 25 people who can give me career advice and referrals. (BUILD)   5 4 3 2 1

20. I don't mind approaching people with my professional concerns. (CONNECT/BUILD)   5 4 3 2 1

21. I enjoy having others contribute to my success. (BUILD)   5 4 3 2 1

22. When I have a problem or face a challenge, I usually contact someone for information and advice. (BUILD)   5 4 3 2 1

23. I'm good at asking questions and getting useful advice from others. (BUILD)   5 4 3 2 1

24. I usually handle rejections in stride by learning from them and moving on. (BUILD)   5 4 3 2 1

25. I can sketch a diagram, with appropriate linkages, of individuals who are most important in both my personal and professional networks. (BUILD)   5 4 3 2 1

26. I regularly do online networking by participating in Usenet newsgroups, mailing lists, chats, and bulletin boards. (CONNECT/BUILD)   5 4 3 2 1

27. I regularly communicate my accomplishments to key members of my network. (NURTURE)   5 4 3 2 1

28. I make it a habit to stay in touch with members of my network by telephone, e-mail, and letter. (NURTURE)   5 4 3 2 1

29. I regularly send personal notes, birthday and holiday greeting cards, and letters on special occasions to people in my network. (NURTURE)   5 4 3 2 1

30. I still stay in touch with childhood friends and old schoolmates. (NURTURE)   5 4 3 2 1

31. I have a great network of individuals whom I can call on at anytime for assistance, and they will be happy to help me. (BUILD/NURTURE)   5 4 3 2 1

32. I belong to several organizations, including a professional association. (CONNECT/BUILD)   5 4 3 2 1

33. I consider myself an effective networker who never abuses my relationships. (CONNECT/BUILD/NURTURE)   5 4 3 2 1

34. Others see me as a savvy networker. (CONNECT/BUILD/NURTURE)   5 4 3 2 1

TOTAL NETWORKING I.Q.

If your total composite I.Q. is above 160, you're most likely a savvy networker. If you're below 125, you're probably lacking key networking skills. Each of the above items indicates a particular connect, build, or nurture behavior or skill that contributes to one's overall networking effectiveness. Concentrate on improving those skills on which you appear to be weak. For example, you may discover you are particularly savvy at "connecting" with people, but you're weak on "building" and "nurturing" relationships – or vice versa – that define your network.

TIP #100
Make networking a centerpiece activity throughout your job search.

Studies consistently show that formal and impersonal communications are the least effective means of getting a job: advertisements, public and private employment agencies, and job listings provided by organizations. The most widely used and effective methods are informal and involve personal relationships: **personal contacts and direct applications**. Indeed, the personal contact is the major job-finding method, used by nearly 75 percent of all job seekers.

Studies also note that **both** employers and employees **prefer** the informal and personal methods.

> *The personal contact is the major job-finding method, used by nearly 75 percent of all successful job seekers.*

Both groups believe personal contacts result in more in-depth, accurate, and up-to-date information which both groups need. Employers feel these methods **reduce their recruiting costs and hiring risks**. Individuals who use personal contacts are more **satisfied** with their jobs; those who find jobs using formal methods tend to have a greater degree of job dissatisfaction. Those using informal methods tend to have **higher incomes**.

Since we know most good jobs are found through networking, it's important that you get on with the business of networking in a very big way. Don't just acknowledge networking as being important to a job search and then slip back into the habit of focusing primarily on the advertised job market. Make networking the centerpiece activity in your job search from day one. Networking should result in providing you with important information about the job market, alternative jobs and careers, employers, companies, and individuals. As such, networking is central to any research campaign. It will help you uncover job leads as well as communicate your qualifications to potential employers who are looking for individuals with your particular mix of interests, skills, abilities, personality, and energy.

TIP #101
Develop a clear understanding of networking, but be sure to practice it on a daily basis.

Here's one of the most disappointing and frustrating behaviors I constantly observe among job seekers. Many job seekers have a clear understanding of the networking process – its central importance, how it works, and how to do it – but they fail to organize and implement an effective networking campaign. They may get started by contacting a few friends for information, advice, and referrals, but they soon fall back on old habits

> *The reluctance to network goes back to some cultural issues related to childhood.*

that seem less risky and more assuring – respond to classified ads with resumes and letters. Part of this reluctance to engage in an active networking campaign goes back to some cultural issues related to childhood – don't talk to strangers nor be too assertive or personal among friends. Many people also are reluctant to make cold calls because they fear encountering rejections (Tip #24). If these are issues preventing you from developing an effective networking campaign in your job search, I recommend the following books and audiotapes to help you develop the necessary skills and motivation to network:

The Savvy Networker: Building Your Job Net for Success
(Ron and Caryl Krannich, both book and audiotape)
Networking for Job and Career Success (L. Michelle Tullier)

A Foot in the Door: Networking Your Way Into the
    Hidden Job Market (Katharine Hansen)
Networking Smart (Wayne E. Baker)
Masters of Networking (Ivan R. Misner, Don Morgan, et al.)
How to Work a Room (Susan RoAne)
Power Networking (Donna and Sandy Vilas)
The Power to Get In (Michael A. Boylan)
Dig Your Well Before You're Thirsty (Harvey Mackay)
Make Your Contacts Count (Anne Baber and Lynne Waymon)

TIP #102
Make sure your networking involves three major activities – building, expanding, and nurturing your network.

Networking involves much more than just making contacts. Be sure your networking campaign focuses on building, expanding, and nurturing your networks (see my notes next to each I.Q. item on pages 148-150). You **build** your network by developing a contact list – it may include friends, relatives, neighbors, classmates, co-workers, and professional associates – and contacting them for information, advice, and referrals. You **expand** your network by following up on referrals and making cold calls that result in linking your network to networks of other individuals. You **nurture** your networks by staying in contact, thanking individuals for their assistance, and doing good deeds and returning favors to those who remain a part of your network. If you fail to properly nurture your network, you'll quickly become a one-time networker who primarily used other people to get ahead. A network is something you need to constantly build, expand, and nurture for your long-term personal and professional success.

TIP #103
Cast as large a net as possible in your job search.

The larger your net, the more useful information, advice, and referrals you will receive on the hidden job market. If you make five new contacts a day, for example, you'll produce over 30 fresh contacts a week. Multiply those numbers by a typical three- to six-month job search or increase the level of your daily networking activities and you will soon have hundreds of individuals involved in your job search. As you link your network to others' networks, you'll build a huge network of individuals who will assist you in various phases of your job search.

TIP #104
Avoid 10 common networking errors.

Many job seekers commit a variety of networking errors that all but terminate an otherwise useful networking campaign. Don't catch yourself doing the following:

1. Unable to implement by failing to develop and sustain a well organized and targeted campaign for building, expanding, and nurturing one's network of relationships.

2. Become a networking pest, similar to direct-sales people who are constantly in one's face trying to sell products.

3. Contact the wrong people or engage in networking activities with losers who have very little to offer a job seeker.

4. Confuse networking with taking advantage of people.

5. Turn off potential networking contacts by asking them for a job rather than for information, advice, and referrals.

6. Lie about one's true intentions in making a contact and asking for referrals.

7. Exploit relationships for personal gain rather than for mutual support.

8. Fail to express one's gratitude for the contact's time and assistance.

9. Abuse a contact's time and relationships.

10. Believe one must be aggressive and obnoxious rather than pleasant, persistent, and professional when networking.

TIP #105
Include an active online networking campaign.

Networking is increasingly taking on new communication forms in today's high-tech world. Job seekers can take advantage of several websites and electronic databases for conducting a job search, from gathering information on the job market to disseminating resumes to employers. The Internet also allows job seekers to network for information, advice, and job leads. If you belong to one of the major Internet service providers, such as America Online, or have an Internet connection, you can use mailing lists, news groups, bulletin boards, blogs, chat groups, message boards, social networking sites, and email to gather job information and make contacts with potential employers. Using email, you can make personal contacts that give you job leads for further networking via computer or through the more traditional networking methods outlined in this chapter.

Several websites will help you develop networking skills as well as put you in contact with important employment-related networks. These sites include a wealth of information on the networking process:

- **Monster.com** — http://network.monster.com
- **Quintessential Careers** — www.quintcareers.com/networking.html
- **Riley Guide** — www.rileyguide.com/netintv.html
- **Susan RoAne** — www.susanroane.com/free.html
- **Contacts Count** — www.contactscount.com

Once you begin the process of developing your networks, you may want to use the following websites to locate long-lost friends, classmates, and others who might be helpful in your networking campaign:

- **AnyWho** — www.anywho.com
- **Classmates** — www.classmates.com
- **InfoSpace** — www.infospace.com

- KnowX   www.knowx.com
- MyLife.com   www.mylife.com
- Switchboard   www.switchboard.com
- The Ultimate White Pages   www.theultimates.com/white
- People Search Lycos   www.whowhere.com
- Yahoo! People Search   http://people.yahoo.com

If you have military experience and wish to locate some of your former military buddies, be sure to explore these people finders for locating military personnel:

- GI Search.com   www.gisearch.com
- Military.com   www.military.com
- Military Connections   www.militaryconnections.com
- Military USA   www.militaryusa.com

If you've lost contact with your former classmates, try these websites for locating alumni groups:

- Alumni.net   www.alumni.net
- Curious Cat Alumni
  Connections   www.curiouscat.net/alumni

Many women's groups organize networking opportunities among their members for career development purposes. The following organizations are especially relevant to female networkers:

- Advancing Women   www.advancingwomen.com
- American Association of
  University Women   www.aauw.org
- Systers   http://anitaborg.org/initiatives/
                                 systers

- National Association of
  Female Executives   www.nafe.com
- Federally Employed
  Women   www.few.org
- iVillage   www.ivillage.com
- womanowned.com   www.womanowned.com

Business professionals will find these three networking groups of special interest because they sponsor special online and offline networking events:

- **Company of Friends**   http://fastcompany.com/cof
- **ExecuNet**   www.execunet.com
- **Technology Executives**
  Networking Group   www.theteng.org

Many of the large Internet employment sites maintain message boards. Two of the largest message board operations, which offer opportunities to network for information and advice, are:

- **Monster.com**   http://monster.prospero.com/
                                  monsterindex
- **Vault.com**   www.vault.com/wps/portal/na/
                                  boards

The latest trend or fad in online networking is based upon the "six degrees of separation theory" – everyone is connected to everyone else in the world by only six other people. A somewhat dubious theory, nonetheless, these networks have been responsible for a great deal of news media hype since 2003 on how to expand one's network of connections for personal and professional purposes. It's in part responsible for the recent dramatic growth in social networking websites and predictions that such networking websites will eventually lead to the demise of traditional online job board as Web 2.0/Job Search 2.0 evolves (see my comments and reference on page 130). Building electronic communities, such networks are designed to put users into contact with thousands of other people for all types of purposes – from dating to making friends to finding a job to recruiting to developing sales forces to closing business deals. The ultimate soft approach to cold calling, these electronic networks tend to be of questionable value to job seekers who have actually used them. After all, they formalize what is essentially an informal, personal process that works best in one degree removed face-to-face situations. Even so, these new electronic networks offer some interesting online networking opportunities for those who have the time and dedication to make them work. They probably are most effective for those who need to prospect for new business and potential sales contacts, which is the direction many of the more entrepreneurial such networks now take. The following websites are devoted to promoting this type of networking activity:

- LinkedIn   www.linkedin.com
- MySpace   www.myspace.com
- Facebook   www.facebook.com
- Friendster   www.friendster.com
- Ryze Business Networking   http://new.ryze.com/networks/php
- Spoke   www.spoke.com

The first website, www.linkedin.com, tends to be used by more job seekers and recruiters than the other sites. If you want to try your luck with this type of online networking in your job search, or if you are a recruiter seeking new talent, I recommend starting with LinkedIn.

The Internet can significantly enhance your job search. It offers new networking possibilities for individuals who are literate in today's digital technology. If you have access to the Internet, I recommend getting your resume into various employment websites (Tip #85). Explore their job vacancies, resources, chat groups, and message boards. Within a few minutes of electronic networking, you may pick up important job information, advice, and leads that could turn into a real job.

> *The Internet offers new networking possibilities for individuals who are literate in today's digital technology.*

TIP #106
Schedule numerous interviews as you practice the 5Rs of informational interviewing.

An informational interview is a low-stress, face-to-face meeting with a contact or potential employer for the purposes of acquiring the following benefits:

1. **Information** on present or future job opportunities in your interest and skill areas.

2. **Advice** on your job search campaign.

3. **Referrals** to other people who might be able to give you more information, advice, and referrals, which, in turn, may lead to job interviews and offers.

If approached in the proper manner, at least 50 percent of your prospecting and networking activities should result in informational interviews either over the telephone or in face-to-face meetings. Some might prefer to conduct this interview via email. While a face-to-face meeting is preferable to a telephone or email informational interview, be prepared to settle for a telephone or email interview in cases where the individual is too busy to schedule a meeting. Face-to-face meetings with every prospect is an unnecessary waste of time for both you and your prospect. Such meetings take a great deal of time, much of which might be better spent on the telephone. Save face-to-face meeting times for people who really count in your network – the ones who are likely to generate job interviews.

When initiating your networking activities, keep in mind that informational interviews have six major purposes:

1. **Gather current information** on the job market relevant to your specific interests (labor market conditions, potentially interested employers, trends).

2. **Acquire data** on any known specific vacancies (nature of work, job titles, working environment, interpersonal and political climates).

3. **Inform** your contact of your interests and qualifications as well as get his or her reaction to your resume.

4. **Get advice** on how to proceed with your job search, especially relating to specific individuals and companies.

5. **Obtain one or more referrals** to others who can give you additional information and advice on potential vacancies and job market conditions.

6. **Be remembered** for future reference.

You should conduct informational interviews with two audiences: (1) individuals with useful occupational information, and (2) potential employers.

The guiding principle behind networking and informational interviews is this:

The best way to get a job is to ask for job information, advice, and referrals; never ask for a job.

Remember, you want your prospects to engage in the 5Rs of informational interviewing:

- **Reveal** useful information and advice.
- **Refer** you to others.
- **Read** your resume.
- **Revise** your resume.
- **Remember** you for future reference.

If you network according to this principle, you should join the ranks of thousands of successful job seekers who have experienced the 5Rs of informational interviewing. Largely avoiding the advertised job market, you may find your perfect job through such powerful networking activities.

10

Interviewing Tips

T HE JOB INTERVIEW IS the single most important step to getting the job offer. No job interview, no job offer. Everything you have done thus far should have prepared you well for one of the most stressful encounters in your job search. Since this is the most important step, you need to treat it as such. Prepare for the job interview as if it were a $1 million prize. After all, depending how long you work for this company, the job could well generate $1 million in income.

Preparation is the key to a successful job interview. While you can anticipate the interview setting and the types of questions you may be asked, there are many other variables that determine whether or not you will be offered the job – your competition, how well you handle unanticipated behavioral and situational interview questions, and your compensation requirements. In the end, the employer must like you because you impress upon him or her that you will be a good fit for the job. You will bring to the job greater value than the other candidates.

The following tips constitute a quick primer on how to best interview for the job. If you learn only one thing from this chapter, it's preparation, preparation, and preparation!

TIP #107
Test Your Interview I.Q.

While effective resumes, letters, and networking are keys to getting job interviews, you must perform well in the interview in order to get the job offer. Just how well prepared are you? Respond to the following statements by indicating your degree of agreement:

SCALE: 5 = Strongly agree   2 = Disagree
4 = Agree   1 = Strongly disagree
3 = Maybe, not certain

1. I know what skills I can offer employers.	5	4	3	2	1
2. I know what skills employers most seek in candidates.	5	4	3	2	1
3. I can clearly explain to employers what I do well and enjoy doing.	5	4	3	2	1
4. I can explain in 60 seconds why an employer should hire me.	5	4	3	2	1
5. I can identify and target employers I want to get an interview with.	5	4	3	2	1
6. I can develop a job referral network.	5	4	3	2	1
7. I can prospect for job leads.	5	4	3	2	1
8. I can generate at least one job interview for every 10 job search contacts I make.	5	4	3	2	1
9. I can follow up on job interviews.	5	4	3	2	1
10. I can persuade an employer to renegotiate my salary after six months on the job.	5	4	3	2	1
11. I know which questions interviewers are most likely to ask me.	5	4	3	2	1
12. If asked to reveal my weaknesses, I know how to respond – answer honestly, but always stress my strengths.	5	4	3	2	1

13. I know how to best dress for the interview.   5   4   3   2   1

14. I know the various types of interviews I may
     encounter and how to appropriately respond
     in each situation.   5   4   3   2   1

15. I can easily approach strangers for job
     information and advice.   5   4   3   2   1

16. I know where to find information on
     organizations that are most likely to be
     interested in my skills.   5   4   3   2   1

17. I know how to go beyond vacancy announce-
     ments to locate job opportunities appropriate
     for my qualifications.   5   4   3   2   1

18. I know how to interview appropriate
     people for job information and advice.   5   4   3   2   1

19. I know many people who can refer me to
     others for informational interviews.   5   4   3   2   1

20. I can uncover jobs on the hidden job market.   5   4   3   2   1

21. I know how to prepare and practice for the
     critical job interview.   5   4   3   2   1

22. I know how to stress my positives.   5   4   3   2   1

23. I know how to research the organization and
     individuals who are likely to interview me.   5   4   3   2   1

24. I have considered how I would respond to
     illegal questions posed by prospective
     employers.   5   4   3   2   1

25. I can telephone effectively for job leads.   5   4   3   2   1

26. I am prepared to conduct an effective
     telephone interview.   5   4   3   2   1

27. I know when and how to deal with salary
     questions.   5   4   3   2   1

28. I know what to read while waiting in the
     outer office prior to the interview.   5   4   3   2   1

29. I can nonverbally communicate my interest
    and enthusiasm for the job.   5   4   3   2   1

30. I know the best time to arrive at the
    interview site.   5   4   3   2   1

31. I know how to respond using positive form
    and content as well as supports when
    responding to interviewers' questions.   5   4   3   2   1

32. I know how to summarize my strengths
    and value at the closing of the interview.   5   4   3   2   1

33. I know what to include in a thank-you letter.   5   4   3   2   1

34. I know when and how to follow up the
    job interview.   5   4   3   2   1

35. I know what do during the 24- to 48-hour
    period following a job offer.   5   4   3   2   1

36. I can clearly explain to interviewers what
    I like and dislike about particular jobs.   5   4   3   2   1

37. I can explain to interviewers why I made
    my particular educational choices, including
    my major and grade point average.   5   4   3   2   1

38. I can clearly explain to interviewers what
    I want to be doing 5 or 10 years from now.   5   4   3   2   1

39. I have a list of references who can speak in
    a positive manner about me and my work
    abilities.   5   4   3   2   1

40. I can clearly state my job and career
    objectives as both skills and outcomes.   5   4   3   2   1

41. I have set aside 20 hours a week to primarily
    conduct informational interviews.   5   4   3   2   1

42. I know what foods and drinks are best to
    select if the interview includes a luncheon
    or dinner meeting.   5   4   3   2   1

43. I know how to listen effectively.   5   4   3   2   1

44.	I can explain why an employer should hire me.	5	4	3	2	1
45.	I am prepared to handle the salary question at whatever point it comes up.	5	4	3	2	1
46.	I know when to use my resume in an informational interview.	5	4	3	2	1
47.	I can generate three new job leads each day.	5	4	3	2	1
48.	I can outline my major achievements in my last three jobs and show how they relate to the job I am interviewing for.	5	4	3	2	1
49.	I know what the interviewer is looking for when he or she asks about my weaknesses.	5	4	3	2	1
50.	I am prepared to handle panel, serial, stress, behavioral, and situational interviews.	5	4	3	2	1

TOTAL I.Q. [   ]

Once you have completed this exercise, add your responses to compute a total score. This will comprise your composite I.Q. If your score is between 200 and 250, you seem well prepared to successfully handle the interview. If your score is between 150 and 199, you are heading in the right direction, and many of my recommended resources should help you increase your interview competencies. If your score falls below 150, you have a great deal of work to do in preparation for the job interview.

TIP #108
Avoid common interview errors.

Unlike many other job search mistakes, interview errors tend to be unforgiving. This is the time when **first impressions** count the most.

Employers have both positive and negative goals in mind. On the positive side, they want to hire someone who can do the job and add value or benefits to their organization. On the negative side, they are always looking for clues that tell them why they should **not** hire you.

After all, you are probably another stranger who makes inflated claims about your competence in the hope of getting a job offer. It's not until you start performing on the job that the employer gets to see the "real you" and discover your patterns of behavior. In the meantime, the employer needs to be on his or her guard looking for evidence that you may be the wrong person for the job. Make a mistake during the job interview and you may be instantly eliminated from further consideration. Therefore, you must be on your very best behavior and avoid the many common mistakes interviewees make.

The following mistakes are frequently cited by employers who have interviewed hundreds of applicants:

1. **Arrives late to the interview.** First impressions really do count and they are remembered for a long time. Arrive late and you've made one of the worst impressions possible! Indeed, regardless of what you say or do during the interview, you may never recover from this initial mistake. Employers wonder *"Will you also come to work late?"*

2. **Makes a bad impression in the waiting area.** Treats receptionists and secretaries as inferiors – individuals who may have important input into the hiring process when later asked by the employer *"What was your impression of this candidate?"* Caught reading frivolous materials – *People Magazine* – in the waiting area when company reports and related literature were readily available.

3. **Offers stupid excuses for behavior.** Excuses are usually red flags indicating that a person is unwilling to take responsibility and do the work. Here's a killer excuse for arriving late for a job interview: *"I got lost because your directions weren't very clear."* Goodbye! Here are some other classic excuses heard during job interviews:

    - *I forgot.*
    - *It wasn't my fault.*
    - *It was a bad company.*
    - *My boss was a real jerk.*
    - *The college wasn't very good.*
    - *I can't remember why I did that.*
    - *No one there appreciated my work.*
    - *I didn't have time to visit your website.*
    - *I'm not a job hopper – I'm getting lots of experience.*

4. **Presents a poor appearance and negative image.** Dresses inappropriately for the interview – under-dresses or over-dresses for the position. He or she may need to learn some basic grooming habits, from haircut and style to makeup and nails, or undergo a major makeover.

5. **Expresses bad, negative, and corrosive attitudes.** Tends to be negative, overbearing, very aggressive, cynical, and opinionated to the extreme. Expresses intolerance and strong prejudices toward others. Complains a lot about everything and everybody. Reveals a possible caustic personality that will not fit in well with the company. Regardless of how talented this person may be, unless he works in a cell by himself, he'll probably be fired within two months for having a bad attitude that pollutes the office and harms morale.

6. **Engages in inappropriate and unexpected behaviors for an interview situation.** Shows off scars, tattoos, muscles, or pictures of family. Flirts with the interviewer. Possibly an exhibitionist who may also want to date the boss and harass co-workers!

7. **Appears somewhat incoherent and unfocused.** Tends to offer incomplete thoughts, loses focus, and jumps around to unrelated ideas. Hard to keep a focused conversation going. Incoherent thought processes indicate a possible attention deficit disorder (ADD) problem.

8. **Inarticulate.** Speaks poorly, from sound of voice and diction to grammar, vocalized pauses, and jargon. Uses lots of _"you know,"_ _"ah,"_ _"like,"_ _"okay,"_ and _"well"_ fillers. Expresses a low class street language – _"cool,"_ _"damn,"_ _"man,"_ _"wow."_ Not a good candidate for using the telephone or interacting with clients. Appears verbally illiterate.

9. **Gives short and incomplete answers to questions.** Tends to respond to most questions with _"Yes,"_ _"No,"_ _"Maybe,"_ or _"I'm not sure"_ when the interviewer expects more in-depth answers. Appears shallow and indicates a lack of substance, initiative, interest, and enthusiasm.

10. **Lacks a sense of direction.** Appears to have no goals or apparent objectives. Just looking for a job and paycheck rather than pursuing a passion or cause.

11. **Appears ill or has a possible undisclosed medical condition.** Looks pale, glassy-eyed, gaunt, or yellow. Coughs, sneezes, and

sounds terrible. Talks about her upcoming operation – within six weeks of starting the job! Suspects this person may have an illness or a drug and alcohol addiction.

12. **Volunteers personal information that normally would be illegal or inappropriate to ask.** Candidate makes interviewer feel uncomfortable by talking about religion, politics, age, family, divorce, sexual orientation, or physical and mental health.

13. **Emits bad or irritating smells.** Reeks of excessive perfume, cologne, or shaving lotion – could kill mosquitos! Can smell smoke or alcohol on breath. Strong body odor indicates personal hygiene problems. Has bad breath throughout the interview, which gets cut short by the employer for an unexplained reason!

14. **Shows little enthusiasm, drive, or initiative.** Appears to be just looking for a job and a paycheck. Tends to be passive and indifferent. No evidence of being a self-starter who takes initiative and solves problems on his own. Not sure what motivates this person other than close supervision. Indeed, he'll require lots of supervision or the company will have an employee with lots of play-time on his hands or the job will expand to fill the time allotted. He'll become the "job guy" who always says *"I did my job just like you told me,"* but not much beyond what's assigned. Don't expect much from this person, who will probably be overpaid for what he produces.

15. **Lacks confidence and self-esteem.** Seems very unsure of self, nervous, and ill at ease. Lacks decisiveness in making decisions. Communicates uncertainly with such comments as *"I don't know," "Maybe," "I'm not sure," "Hadn't really thought of that," "Interesting question," "I'll have to think about that,"* or redirects with the question *"Well, what do you think?"*

16. **Appears too eager and hungry for the job.** Is overly enthusiastic, engages in extreme flattery, and appears suspiciously nervous. Early in the interview, before learning much about the company or job, makes such comments as *"I really like it here," "I need this job," "Is there overtime?," "What are you paying?," "How many vacation days do you give?"*

17. **Communicates dishonesty or deception.** Uses canned interview language, evades probing questions, and appears disingenuous. Looks like a tricky character who has things to hide and thus will probably be sneaky and deceptive on the job.

18. **Feels too smooth and superficial.** Dresses nicely, has a firm handshake and good eye contact, answers most questions okay, and appears enthusiastic – just like the books tell job seekers to do. But when asked more substantive *"What if"* and behavior-based questions, or requested to give examples of specific accomplishments, the candidate seems to be caught off balance and stumbles, giving incomplete answers. Can't put one's finger on the problem, but the gut reaction is that this role-playing candidate is very superficial and will probably end up being the "dressed for success" and "coached for the interview" employee from hell!

19. **Appears evasive when asked about possible problems with background.** Gives elusive answers to red flag questions about frequent job changes, termination, and time gaps in work history. Such answers raise concerns about the interviewee's honesty, credibility, responsibility, and overall behavior. Indicates a possible negative behavior pattern that needs further investigation.

20. **Speaks negatively of previous employers and co-workers.** When asked why she left previous employers, usually responds by bad-mouthing them. Has little good to say about others who apparently were not as important as this candidate.

21. **Maintains poor eye contact.** At least in America, eye contact is an indication of trustworthiness and attention. Individuals who fail to maintain an appropriate amount of eye contact are often judged as untrustworthy – have something to hide. Having too little or too much eye contact during the interview gives off mixed messages about what you are saying. Worst of all, it may make the interviewer feel uncomfortable in your presence.

22. **Offers a limp or overly firm handshake.** Interviewers often get two kinds of handshakes from candidates – the wimps and the bone-crushers. Your initial handshake may say something about your personality. Candidates offering a cold, wet, and limp handshake often come across as corpses! Bone-crushers may appear too aggressive.

23. **Shows little interest in the company.** Indicates he didn't do much research, since he knows little about the company and didn't have time to check out the company's website. Asks this killer question: *"What do you do here?"*

24. **Talks about salary and benefits early in the interview.** Rather than try to learn more about the company and position as

well as demonstrate her value, the candidate seems preoccupied with salary and benefits by talking about them within the first 15 minutes of the interview. Shows little interest in the job or employer beyond the compensation package. When the interviewee prematurely starts to talk about compensation, red flags go up again – this is a self-centered candidate who is not really interested in doing the job or advancing a career.

25. **Is discourteous, ill-mannered, and disrespectful.** Arrives for the interview a half hour late with no explanation or a phone call indicating a problem en route. Just sits and waits for the interviewer to ask questions. Picks up things on the interviewer's desk. Bites nails and picks nose during the interview. Challenges the interviewer's ideas. Closes the interview without thanking the interviewer for the opportunity to interview for the job. Not even going to charm and etiquette school would help this candidate!

26. **Tells inappropriate jokes and laughs a lot.** Attempts at humor bomb – appears to be a smart ass who likes to laugh at his own jokes. Comes across as an irritating clown who says stupid and silly things. Will need to frequently put this one out to pasture to keep him away from other employees who don't share such humor.

27. **Talks too much.** Can't answer a question without droning on and on with lots of irrelevant talk. Volunteers all kinds of information, including interesting but sensitive personal observations and gossip, the interviewer neither needs nor wants. Doesn't know when to shut up. Would probably waste a lot of valuable work time talking, talking, and talking and thus irritating other employees. Seems to need lots of social strokes through talk, which she readily initiates.

28. **Drops names to impress the interviewer.** Thinks the interviewer will be impressed with a verbal Rolodex of who he knows. But interviewers tend to be put off with such candidates who, instead, appear insecure, arrogant, and patronizing – three deadly sins that may shorten your interview from 45 minutes to 15 minutes!

29. **Appears needy and greedy.** Talks a lot about financial needs and compensation. When discussing salary, talks about his personal financial situation, including debts and planned future purchases, rather than what the job is worth and what value he will bring to the job. Seems to expect the employer to be interested in supporting his lifestyle, which may be a combination of irresponsible financial behavior, failing to plan, living beyond his

pay grade, and having bad luck. This line of talk indicates he probably has debilitating financial problems that go far beyond the salary level of this job.

30. **Closes the interview by just leaving.** Most interviewees fail to properly close interviews. How you close the interview may determine whether or not you will be invited back to another interview or offered the job. Never ever close the interview with this stupid and presumptuous closing prior to being offered the job: *"So when can I start?"* This question will finish off the interview and your candidacy – you're back to being needy and greedy! Also, don't play the pressure game, even if it's true, by stating *"I have another interview this week. When can I expect to hear from you?"* One other critical element to this close: send a nice thank-you letter within 24 hours in which you again express your appreciation for the interview and your interest in the job.

31. **Fails to talk about accomplishments.** Candidate concentrates on explaining work history as primarily consisting of assigned duties and responsibilities. When asked to give examples of her five major accomplishments in her last jobs, doesn't seem to understand the question, gives little evidence of performance, or reverts once again to discussing formal duties and responsibilities. When probed further for accomplishments, doesn't really say much and shows discomfort about this line of questioning.

32. **Does not ask questions about the job or employer.** When asked *"Do you have any questions?,"* candidate replies *"No"* or *"You've covered everything."* Asking questions is often more important than answering questions. When you ask thoughtful questions, you emphasize your interest in the employer and job as well as indicate your intelligence – qualities employers look for in candidates.

33. **Appears self-centered rather than employer-centered.** This will become immediately apparent by the direction of the answers and questions coming from the interviewee. If the candidate primarily focuses on benefits to him, he will be perceived as self-centered. For example, a candidate who frequently uses "I" when talking about himself and the job may be very self-centered. On the other hand, the candidate who talks about "we" and "you" is usually more employer-oriented. Contrast these paired statements about the job and compensation:

"What would I be doing in this position?"

"What do you see us achieving over the next six months?"

or

"What would I be making on this job?"

"What do you normally pay for someone with my qualifications?"

34. **Demonstrates poor listening skills.** Doesn't listen carefully to questions or seems to have her own agenda that overrides the interviewer's interest. Tends to go off in different directions from the questions being asked. Not a very empathetic listener both verbally and nonverbally. Seems to be more interested in talking about own agenda than focusing on the issues at hand. Apparently wants to take charge of the interview and be the Lone Ranger. The job really does require good listening skills!

35. **Seems not too bright for the job.** Answering simple interview questions is like giving an intelligence test. Has difficulty talking about past accomplishments. Doesn't seem to grasp what the job is all about or the skills required. Seems confused and lacks focus. Should never have gotten to the job interview but had a terrific looking resume that was probably written by a professional resume writer!

36. **Fails to know his/her worth and negotiate properly when it comes time to talk about compensation.** Job seekers are well advised to only talk about salary and benefits **after** being offered the job. If you prematurely talk about compensation, you may diminish your value as well as appear self-centered. Be sure to research salary comparables so you know what you are worth in today's job market (start with www.salary.com). Listen carefully throughout the interview and ask questions that would give you a better idea of what the job is actually worth. Stress throughout the interview your skills and accomplishments – those things that are most valued by employers who are willing to pay what's necessary for top talent. When you do start negotiating, let the employer state a salary figure first and then negotiate using salary ranges to reach common ground.

37. **Fails to properly prepare for the interview.** This is the most important mistake of all. It affects all the other mistakes. Indeed, failing to prepare will immediately show when the candidate makes a bad first impression, fails to indicate knowledge about the company and job, poorly answers standard interview questions, and does not ask questions. In other words, the candidate

makes many of the mistakes outlined above because he or she failed to anticipate what goes into a winning interview.

TIP #109
Use both print and online resources to prepare for the job interview.

If you need help in preparing for the job interview, I recommend the following print and Internet resources:

Books

101 Dynamite Questions to Ask at Your Job Interview (Richard Fein)
101 Great Answers to the Toughest Interview Questions (Ron Fry)
250 Job Interview Questions You'll Most Likely Be Asked (Peter Veruki)
Adams Job Interview Almanac, with CD-ROM (Adams Media)
Best Answers to 202 Job Interview Questions (Daniel Porot and Frances Bolles Haynes
I Can't Believe They Asked Me That! (Ron and Caryl Krannich)
Interview Rehearsal Book (Deb Gottesman and Buzz Mauro)
Job Interview Tips for People With Not-So-Hot Backgrounds (Ron and Caryl Krannich)
Job Interviews for Dummies (Joyce Lain Kennedy)
KeyWords to Nail Your Job Interview (Wendy S. Enelow)
Nail the Job Interview! (Caryl and Ron Krannich)
Naked at the Interview (Burton Jay Nadler)
Power Interviews (Neil M. Yeager and Lee Hough)
Savvy Interviewing (Ron and Caryl Krannich)
You Should Hire Me! (Ron and Caryl Krannich)

Websites

- Monster.com   http://career-advice.monster.com
- InterviewPro   www.interviewpro.com
- JobInterview.net   www.job-interview.net
- Interview Coach   www.interviewcoach.com

- Quintessential Careers   www.quintcareers.com/intvres.html
- The Riley Guide   www.rileyguide.com/netintv.html
- WSACorp.com   www.WSACorp.com
- About.com   http://jobsearch.about.com/cs/
  interviews/a/jobinterviewtip.htm

TIP #110
Approach the interview as an important information exchange.

Most people still view interview success in narrow terms: success is to get a job offer. But to get the job offer is only one of many outcomes of the employment interview which may or may not be positive for you. Only time and experience on the job will tell you if getting the job was a good idea.

Success may mean learning the position is not for you.

An important goal and outcome of any job interview should be to **obtain useful information** to determine whether the job is right for you. Success in the interview may mean learning that the position is **not** for you, and thus you turn down the job offer. Or perhaps the offer is not made since the interviewer also realizes the job is not a good fit for you. If you view a major goal of your interview to be gathering information, you will most likely perform better in the interview situation. Rather than feel you are in a stressful win-lose game, you will be more at ease as you focus on what the interview is all about – **an exchange of useful information between the interviewer and interviewee**. It is to your advantage to make sure this exchange takes place in your favor. You gain information about the job and present yourself, with honesty, in the most positive way possible.

Another successful outcome would be to market yourself for future positions in this or other organizations. The interview could establish a good basis for developing a job information and referral network.

I urge you to approach the interview as a two-way street: both you and the employer want to better know each other. While the interviewer is trying to determine whether to hire you, you should be determining whether you want to work for the employer. There is nothing worse than dampening the euphoria of getting the job with the realization two months later that the job is not right for you. So beware of supposedly positive outcomes – job offers – that can lead to negative career experiences!

TIP #111
Expect several interviews with the same employer.

Many interviewees are surprised to learn they are subjected to more than one interview with the same employer. They normally experience two interviews: screening and hiring/placement. The screening interview may take place over the telephone. You must be prepared for that unexpected telephone call in which the employer probes your continuing interest in the position, your availability, and your job-related expectations, including, perhaps, salary requirements. The hiring/placement interview is normally conducted in the interviewer's office. But it may involve a one-to-one interview or sequential, series, panel, or group interviews. This process could take place over a one- or two-week period in which you are called back to meet with other individuals in one-to-one, series, panel, or group interview situations. Each interview may probe a different level of your interests, abilities, knowledge, and skills.

> *Expect to encounter two interviews with the same employer – screening and hiring/placement.*

TIP #112
Prepare for different types of interviews.

Employers conduct eight different types of interviews to determine if candidates are the right fit for their company or organization. The first five interview types relate to the interview setting. The final three types focus on questioning techniques.

The most common types of interviews include:

1. **One-on-one interviews:** This is the traditional entry-level type of interview most job seekers expect – meeting and exchanging information with one individual, the interviewer or employer. This usually takes place at the employer's office where the candidate and employer sit down to discuss the position and the applicant's skills, knowledge, and abilities.

2. **Sequential interviews:** These are a series of interviews with the decision being made to screen the candidate in or out after each interview. With sequential interviews, many employment issues such as salary and benefits may not be discussed in the initial interview. These interviews can work to your advantage – with each interview you should have the opportunity to find out more about the position and ask questions you forgot in previous interviews.

3. **Serial interviews:** Consists of several interviews, one after the other. Usually each meeting is with a different person or group of people, and all the interviews will be held over a one- or two-day period. Following these interviews, the individuals will meet to compare notes and make a group hiring decision.

4. **Panel interviews:** These interviews occur infrequently, but you may encounter them. In a panel interview you are interviewed by several people at the same time. These are among the most stressful interview situations. At its best, you are facing several people at the same time, responding to the questions of one panel member as you try to balance your perceptions of the other members' expectations.

5. **Group interviews:** On occasion you may encounter this type of competitive interview. Here you find yourself being interviewed along with several other applicants. In group interviews the employer will observe the interpersonal skills of the applicants. Often a question will be posed to the group, or the group will be presented with a problem to

solve. At least you'll know your competition when placed in such an interview setting!

6. **Behavioral interviews:** Many employers like to use behavioral interviews because they probe the decision-making skills of candidates and they know candidates cannot prepare well for such interviews. These interviews usually involve self-appraisal questions, situational questions, and hypothetical situational questions. For example, an interviewer might ask, _"In what situations have you become so involved in the work you were doing that the day flew by?"_ If you have been explaining how you handled an irate customer, the interviewer might ask, _"If you were to encounter that same situation now, how would you deal with that customer?"_ Situation questions might include _"Tell me about a recent time when you took responsibility for a task that was outside of your job description."_ Hypothetical situational questions ask the applicant what he would do in a hypothetical situation. Thus they give the interviewer the opportunity to ask questions about situations the applicant may never have actually encountered in a previous position.

7. **Examination/test interviews:** Some interviews will include elements of testing or examination. For some types of jobs, such as clerical or mechanical, you may be tested on the actual equipment you will be using. Teachers may be asked to conduct a one-hour classroom session where their performance will be observed and evaluated by both faculty and students. Certain questions, similar to those outlined in the section on indirect questions, may be asked to ascertain your level of knowledge, decision-making capabilities, analytic capabilities, and competence. _"What if"_ questions that begin with _"What would you do if . . ."_ are designed to test your ability to relate your past experience to the employer's current situation and needs. Using questions designed to test you, interviewers are looking for thoughtful answers that demonstrate your competence.

8. **Situational interviews:** If you watched the popular television program "The Apprentice," you know exactly what a situational interview is all about. More and more employers are using these interviews to screen the actual observed performance of candidates. In a situational interview, a candidate is asked to deal with an actual work-related situation or problem where he or she can be observed making decisions and generating positive or negative outcomes. For example, if you are interviewing for a customer service position, you might be asked to handle a telephone call from an irate customer. You'll be observed trying to solve the customer's problem. How well you handle that customer may well determine whether or not you will be offered the job. Like the behavioral interview, you have difficulty preparing for such an interview. Indeed, employers like these interviews because they can observe the actual behavior of candidates solving problems they will likely encounter on a day-to-day basis.

TIP #113
Anticipate and prepare for questions.

You can anticipate before you even walk into the interview 90-95 percent of the questions you will be asked. You can expect to be asked about your education and work experience as they relate to the job under consideration. You may be asked questions about your personality, work habits, ability to work with others, or your career goals. In addition to the standard areas of inquiry, a look at your resume should tell you if there are areas likely to get the attention of the interviewer. Do you have red flags showing, such as unexplained time gaps in your education or work life? Have you jumped around from employer to employer in a short time period? Are you applying for a position that is significantly below your apparent abilities and previous work experience? Since you will be showcasing your best behavior in the job interview, always anticipate and thoroughly prepare for possible questions.

TIP #114
Prepare to deal with illegal questions.

Title VII of the Civil Rights Act of 1964 makes discrimination on the basis of race, sex, religion, or national origins illegal in personnel decisions. The Americans With Disabilities Act of 1990 includes questions related to disabilities as being illegal. Questions that delve into these areas as well as others, such as age, height, or weight, are also illegal, unless they can be shown to directly relate to bona fide occupational qualifications. If a question relates directly to the job, it is usually legal to ask.

Most interviewers are well aware of these restrictions and will not ask you illegal questions. However, you may still encounter such questions either because of ignorance on the part of the interviewer or blatant violation of the regulations. As I noted earlier when discussing "personal" questions, many interviewers may ask these questions indirectly. However, some interviewers still ask them directly.

Women are more likely to face illegal questions than men. Some employers still ask questions regarding birth control, child care, or how their husbands feel about them working or traveling. The following types of questions are considered illegal:

- Are you married, divorced, separated, single, or gay?
- How old are you?
- Do you go to church regularly?
- Do you have many debts?
- How many children do you have?
- Do you own or rent your home?
- What social or political organizations do you belong to?
- What does your spouse think about your career?
- Are you living with anyone?
- Are you practicing birth control?
- Were you ever arrested?
- What kind of insurance do you carry?
- How much do you weigh?
- How tall are you?
- Do you have any particular disabilities?
- What do your parents do?

- Have you ever been treated for depression?
- Do you ever been diagnosed with ADHD?
- Have you ever sued an employer or co-worker?
- How often do you see a doctor?
- Have you had any mental health or psychiatric problems?

Consider the following options for handling illegal and personal questions. If you encounter such questions, your choice may depend upon which is more important to you: defending a principle or giving yourself the greatest chance to land the job. You may decide the job is not as important as the principle. Or you may decide, even though you really want this job, you could never work in an organization that employed such clods, and tell them so.

On the other hand, you may choose to answer the question, offensive though it may be, because you really want the job. If you get the job, you vow you will work from within the organization to change such interview practices.

There is yet a third scenario here. You may believe the employer is purposefully trying to see how you will react to stressful questions. Will you lose your temper or will you answer meekly? Though a rather dangerous practice for employers, this does occur. In this situation you should remain cool and answer tactfully by indicating indirectly that the questions may be inappropriate.

For example, if you are divorced and the interviewer asks about your divorce, you could respond by asking, *"Does a divorce have a direct bearing on the responsibilities of this position?"*

A possible response to any illegal question – regardless of motive – is to turn what appears to be a negative into a positive. If, for example, you are female and the interviewer asks you how many children you still have living at home and you say, *"I have five – two boys and three girls,"* you can expect this answer will be viewed as a negative. Working mothers with five children at home may be viewed as neither good mothers nor dependable employees. Therefore, you could immediately follow this response with a tactful elaboration that will turn this potential negative into a positive. You might say,

I have five – two boys and three girls. They are wonderful children who, along with my understanding husband, take great care of each other. If I didn't have such a supportive and

caring family, I would never think of pursuing a career in this field. I do want you to know that I keep my personal life separate from my professional life. That's very important to me and my family, and I know it's important to employers. In fact, because of my family situation, I make special arrangements with other family members, friends, and day-care centers to ensure that family responsibilities never interfere with my work. But, more important, I think being a mother and working full time has really given me a greater sense of responsibility, forced me to use my time well, and helped me better organize my life and handle stress. I've learned what's important in both my work and life. I would hope that the fact that I'm both a mother and I'm working – and not a working mother – would be something your company would be supportive of, especially given my past performance and the qualifications I would bring to this job.

TIP #115
Prepare a list of questions you need to ask.

Employers often report they are especially impressed with candidates who ask a few important questions during interviews. They are not impressed with those who interrogate them with many questions! When you ask questions, you indicate interest in the position as well as communicate your professionalism. Be prepared to ask questions relevant to the job, employer, and organization. These questions should be designed to elicit information to help you make a decision as well as demonstrate your interest, intelligence, and enthusiasm for the job. You may want to write out several of these questions on a 3x5 card to help you remember the questions you want to ask. It's okay to refer to the card during the interview. Just mention to the interviewer that *"I have a few questions I wanted to ask you. I made some notes so I would be sure to ask them."* Then take out your notes and ask the questions. This indicates to the interviewer that you are prepared and have specific concerns he or she must also address. Questions you might want to ask about the company would revolve around areas not likely covered in materials you could have read before your interview. You want to know something about the following:

- Stability of the position and firm.
- Opportunities available for advancement.
- Management and decision-making styles – teams, hierarchies, degree of decentralization.
- Degree of autonomy permitted and entrepreneurship encouraged.
- Organizational culture.
- Internal politics.

Your questions may cover some of the following areas of inquiry:

- Why is this position open? Is it a new position? If not, why did the previous person leave? If the person was promoted, what position does that person now hold?

- How important is this position to the organization?

- To what extent does the company promote from within versus hiring from the outside?

- What plans for expansion (or cutbacks) are in the immediate future? What effect will these plans have on the position or the department in which it is located?

- On the average, how long do most employees stay with this company?

- Tell me about what it's really like working here in terms of the people, management practices, workloads, expected performance, and rewards.

- How would you evaluate the financial soundness and growth potential of this company?

- If you had to briefly describe this organization, what would you say? What about its employees? Its managers and supervisors? Its performance evaluation system? Its promotion practices?

- Assuming my work is excellent, where might you see me in another five years within this organization?

Questions about the job will relate more specifically to the day-to-day activities you could expect if you were to join this organization. You may wish to ask about some of the following concerns:

- How did this opening occur? Is it a newly created position or did someone recently leave the position?

- Tell me about the nature of the work I would be doing most of the time.

- What kinds of peripheral tasks would likely take up the balance of my time?

- What would be my most important duties? Responsibilities?

- What types of projects would I be involved with?

- What kinds of clients would I be working with?

- What changes is management interested in having take place within the direction of this department?

- What is the management style of the person who would be my supervisor?

- In what ways is management looking for this function [the function performed by the department I would be working in] to be improved?

- What have been the major problems [barriers to achieving department goals] in the past?

- What will be the major challenges for the person who is hired?

- How often would I be expected to travel?

You also should ask questions about the work environment. Consider asking some of these potentially revealing questions:

- Can you tell me something about the people I would be working with? Working for?

- How is performance evaluated? How often, by whom, what criteria are used? Does the employee have input into the evaluation? Do you have an annual performance appraisal system in place? How long has it been operating? How does it relate to promotions and salary increments? How do employees feel about this system?

- Can you tell me something about the company's management system? How do supervisors see their role in this company? Tell me about the person who would be my immediate supervisor.

- Is there much internal politics that would affect my position? Will I be expected to become part of anyone's group? How controversial is this hiring decision? Who is considered the most influential person in my division?

- Does the company provide in-house training? Does it support employees taking advantage of outside training in areas where it does not provide training programs? Is there support for employees returning to school for additional formal education?

- How open are opportunities for advancement? Assuming high performance, to what other positions might I progress?

TIP #116
Prepare for different questioning techniques.

While you may be prepared to respond to direct questions with direct answers, some interviewers also include indirect and stress questioning techniques. For example, rather than ask *"Do you have difficulty working with your employers?,"* they may ask *"Why did you leave your last three jobs?"* or *"How did you get along with your last three employers?"* Rather than ask you directly about your social status and financial situation, they may ask *"Where do you prefer living in the community?"* If a job involves a great deal of stress, the interviewer may ask you questions that put you under stress during the interview just to see how you handle such situations. For example, you may unexpect- edly be asked *"If we hire you and three months later decide*

> ## Some interviewers include indirect and stress questioning techniques.

you're not the person we want, what are we going to do?" or *"We normally don't hire someone without a college degree. Do you plan to complete college?"* You may very well be thrown questions that are designed to challenge what may be perceived to be your well-rehearsed interview script. Remember, interviewers will be looking for indica- tions of your weaknesses by asking questions that elicit such indica- tors.

TIP #117
Know how to communicate verbally to others.

Strong verbal communication skills are highly valued by most employers. They are signs of educated and competent individuals. Do you, for example, speak in complete and intelligible sentences? How is your diction? Do you say *"going"* rather than *"goin,"* *"going to"* rather than *"gonna,"* *"didn't"* rather than *"din't,"* *"yes"* rather than *"yea"*? Do you have a tendency to use vocalized phases (*"ah"* and *"uhm"*) and fillers (*"you know," "like," "okay"*)? How is your gram- mar? Do you use the active rather than passive voice? Do you avoid using tentative, indecisive terms, such as *"I think," "I guess," "I feel"*? Do you avoid ambiguous and negative terms such as *"pretty good"* or *"fairly well"* which say little if anything? They may even communicate negatives – that what you did was not good!

TIP #118
Know how you communicate
nonverbally to others.

Over 80 percent of what you communicate in the interview is nonverbal. Indeed, as soon as you enter the door, shake hands, sit in the chair, and engage in small talk – usually the first five minutes of the interview – the interviewer has already made up his mind whether or not he likes you. Most of the information being communicated at this point is nonverbal – your appearance, demeanor, smell, feel, facial expressions, and eye contact. If he doesn't initially like you, the remainder of the interview will be a waste of his time. Indeed, you may find the interview will go very fast and you'll be thanked for coming as he closes the interview for good.

So how do you dress, groom, greet, shake hands, use eye contact, sit, maintain posture, use your hands, move your head, maintain facial expressions, listen positively, eat, drink, or enter and leave a room? These are nonverbal behaviors that may communicate more about your competence and personality than what you say in the interview. You may want to videotape yourself in a mock interview to see how well you communicate both verbally and nonverbally. For a complete examination of nonverbal behaviors in the job interview, see Caryl and Ron Krannich's *The Savvy Interviewer: The Nonverbal Advantage* (Impact Publications).

TIP #119
Dress appropriately for the interview.

Before you even open your mouth to speak, your appearance has already made an impression. Since you never get a second chance to make a first impression, make it a good one. Make the first few seconds of the interview work in your favor by nonverbally communicating your class, professionalism, and competence. Always dress appropriately for the occasion, which will vary from one of type of job and organization to another. If you are interviewing for a professional position and most employees are expected to wear business attire, put on your best suit for the interview. If you are interviewing with a company where casual attire is the norm, try to dress one step above the norm. If you are interviewing for a blue collar position where a suit or sport coat would be inappropriate, be sure to dress conservatively and neatly. You don't want your attire to be a distraction – you either over-dressed or under-dressed for the occasion or you simply don't know how to put yourself together with appropriate colors, fabrics, styles, and quality. For useful tips on dress and image, see JoAnna Nicholson's *Dressing Smart for Women* and *Dressing Smart for Men* (Impact Publications).

TIP #120
Be sure to arrive on time.

There's nothing worse than to arrive late for a job interview. Since the first five minutes of the interview are the most important, if you arrive five minutes late, you will effectively kill much of the interview – and your chances of getting the job. Your tardiness will be remembered and in a negative light. Try to arrive at least ten minutes early. If need be, drive to the interview site the day before to estimate how long it will take you to get there as well as find parking. Allow plenty of time, anticipating that you could well lose a half hour or more to bad traffic.

TIP #121
Treat everyone you meet as potentially important to the interview.

When you initially arrive at the interview site, chances are you will enter a reception area, meet a receptionist or secretary, and be asked to sit in that waiting area. Other employees also may enter this area while you are waiting. Make sure you are courteous to the receptionist or secretary and anyone else you meet. Also, you should appear professional in how you greet these people, sit, and what you read. For example, you should greet the receptionist or secretary by introducing yourself: *"Good morning. I'm Jane Morris. I have a 9 o'clock appointment with Mr. Jameson."* Wait to be invited to sit in a specific place. If you are wearing an overcoat, take it off before sitting. Interviewers sometimes ask these employees for their reaction to candidates: *"What did you think about the candidate? Did you have a chance to talk to her? What did she do while she was waiting to meet me? Do you think you'll like her?"* Employees' opinions of such people can be very important to the interview process. So make sure you treat **everyone** you meet as **important** to the interview.

TIP #122
Greet the interviewer properly.

Chances are the interviewer will come out to the reception area to greet you. Stand up straight, shake hands firmly, maintain eye contact, listen carefully, look energetic, speak in the positive, and introduce yourself: *"Hello, I'm Jane Morris. It's a pleasure to meet you."* Watch the small talk carefully. This is not a time to tell dumb jokes, look tired, appear nervous, or say something stupid. If you are asked if you had any trouble finding the place or parking, appear competent and positive by indicating you handled this part of the interview with ease. If you've been so unfortunate as to arrive late for the interview, under no circumstances should you say something stupid like *"Sorry I'm late. I had difficulty finding this place since your directions were not very clear."* Say this and you'll be dead upon arrival!

TIP #123
Communicate positive behaviors during the first five minutes.

The first five minutes of the interview, which may not even address job-related questions, are the most important to the interview. It's during this time that critical first impressions are made and interviewers decide whether or not they like you. And being likable is one of the most important criteria for being selected for a job. If you make an excellent first impression – from shaking hands and dressing right to handling the initial small talk – the rest of the interview may go extremely well as the interviewer helps you through the

> *Make sure your perfume or cologne is applied in moderate amounts and jewelry has been minimized.*

interview. He or she may have decided during the third minute that you should be hired. The questions and answers may merely reinforce these initial impressions. Make sure your perfume or cologne is applied in minimal amounts and jewelry has been minimized. You don't want to be remembered for your strong scent or the noise your clanging jewelry generated! Indeed, many interviewers smell their interviewee as they pass in front of them when entering the interviewer's room.

TIP #124
Let the interviewer initiate the openers, but take initiative in offering some of your own openers.

It is the responsibility of the interviewer to initiate openers. During the first two or three minutes the interviewer will probably talk about your trip to the office, the weather, your impressions of the facilities, or some other small-talk topics. Respond to these questions with more than just "yes" or "no" answers and observations. You need to take some initiative here to express your personality. Initiate your own positive small talk by making an interesting observation about the office, such as the art work or decorating, or

> _The most important impressions are made during the first five minutes. During this time you want to appear energetic, positive, and interesting._

the personnel you met in the reception area. You might, for example, discover from seeing a framed degree hanging on the wall that the interviewer is a graduate of your alma mater. He or she may be a collector of unusual items that are displayed in the office. Or he or she may have an interesting photo displayed of family, friends, colleagues, a ceremony, or someone famous. Show some personal interest in the individual by focusing on one or two items for small talk. This small-talk period may result in building an important **personal bridge** between you and the interviewer that will make this professional encounter a much easier and more enjoyable one. Remember, the most important impressions are made during the first five minutes. You want to appear energetic, positive, and interesting during these initial moments of the interview. In the end, how you handle yourself in the small-talk stage may be as important to getting the job as your responses to the standard interview questions.

TIP #125
Answer questions with complete sentences and with substance.

Avoid simple *"yes"* or *"no"* answers. Remember, the interviewer is looking for **indicators of substance and benefits**. Brief answers give little information about you. They may indicate a lack of interest or substance on your part. The interviewer should leave this interview thinking *"I feel good about this person. He gave good answers to my questions."* If you don't answer the questions completely, how can this person feel good about you?

TIP #126
Be sure to close the interview properly.

Assuming the interview has progressed to its final stage and you have asked questions about the organization, the job, and the work environment, you may breathe a sigh of relief. But you are not finished yet. Remember, you need to ask questions that will establish what you do from here. You do not want to go home and wait for weeks hoping to hear about this job.

Assuming you are still interested in the job, tell that to the interviewer. Ask when she (or the management team) expects to make a decision and when you could expect to hear. Then take the date a day or two after she has indicated a decision should be reached and ask, *"If I haven't heard from you by ____(date)____, may I call you?"* Almost always the interviewer will indicate you may call. Mark the date on your calendar and make certain you do call if you have not heard by then.

This is also a good time to ask the employer if there is any other information they need in order to act on your application. If you still have questions concerning the job, you may want to ask the interviewer if there are two or three present or former employees you might talk to about the organization. He should provide you with the names and phone numbers. Be sure to contact them.

TIP #127
Reduce your nervousness by practicing a few stress reduction techniques.

You can better control your nervousness by following the same advice often given to public speakers. As you walk into the interview room, try to take slow deep breaths. You can do this subtly so the interviewer will be unaware of it. And, although this is easier said than done, the more you can get your mind off yourself and concentrate on the other person, the more comfortable you will feel. If you are nervous, you are probably focusing too much attention on yourself. You are self-consciously concerned with how you are doing and what impression you are making on others. Try to be more other-directed. Rather than concentrate on your needs and fears, concern yourself with the employer's needs and questions. Preparation is probably the greatest aid in lessening nervousness. If you prepared to both answer and ask questions and arrived on time, you should walk into the interview feeling well prepared and confident. If you arrive early for the interview, you will have a chance to collect your thoughts, take those deep breaths, and focus your attention toward the employer.

TIP #128
Emphasize the positive.

You want both the content of your responses and the manner in which you phrase your answers to be positive. As you talk about your previous employer(s), try to cast them in as positive a view as possible. After all, if you talk negatively about a former employer, the prospective employer will assume that someday you'll talk that way about him. If you bad-mouth your former company, the employer will expect that one day you'll do the same to his. If you have only negative remarks about your co-workers, he must question your ability to get along in his organization as well. In other words, you have little to gain – and much to lose – during the interview by venting frustrations about previous jobs.

Try to put on the most positive "spin" possible – honest, but not stupid – as you phrase your responses. Avoid negative words like *"can't," "didn't," "wouldn't,"* and phrase your answers with positive words instead. Rather than say, *"I wouldn't want to travel more than 4-5 days per month,"* you could respond with a more positive, *"I would prefer to keep my travel to 4-5 days per month."* Practice being more positive in your day-to-day communication and you will find it will come to you more easily in an interview.

TIP #129
Turn potential negatives into positives.

While interviewers also want to know what's wrong about you – your negatives – you want to continuously stress your positives – what's right about you. You can do this by maintaining a positive orientation toward all questions.

Most applicants, for example, have some qualification or lack of a qualification that they, as well as potential employers, may consider to be a negative which is likely to knock them out of consideration for the position. Perhaps you are just out of school and hence don't have experience. Maybe you are over 50 and, although you know it is illegal for an employer to discriminate against you on the basis of your age, you believe this will be a hindrance to your getting a job. Perhaps you have not stayed in your past jobs for very long and your resume shows a pattern of job-hopping. Maybe your grades in school were average at best.

Whatever the negatives you believe will hinder your efforts at landing a job, you should attempt to find a way to turn the negative into an honest positive. Take, for example, the case of an older woman – well into her sixties – who came into a personnel office to interview for a newspaper job. The woman evidently thought her age would be a negative, so she came prepared with several advantages to hiring someone her age. Her first advantage was that she *"would not get pregnant!"*

TIP #130
Delay salary considerations as long as possible.

Usually salary is brought up by the interviewer near the end of the first interview, during a second or third interview, or after a job offer has been made. However, some interviewers will bring it up earlier. It is almost always to your advantage to delay discussion of salary as long as possible. In the meantime, you need to do two things:

- Determine the **worth** of the position.

- Demonstrate your **value** to the employer.

You can only do these two things **after** you have had a chance to interview for the position – not at the beginning or in the middle of the interview. You need to have the opportunity to determine what the job is worth based on the duties and responsibilities of the position – something you can best evaluate after you have a chance to ask questions about the position. You also want the opportunity to promote your value to the employer during the give and take of the interview.

Interviewers who bring up salary early – during a telephone screening interview or early in the initial interview – are usually trying to screen people out of consideration based on salary expectations that are either too high or even too low! Attempt to stall by indicating that salary is "open" or that you need to know more about the position before you can discuss salary.

TIP #131
Record information about the interview for your future reference.

Often you will have more than one interview – probably a series – with a company. Make notes while the interview is fresh in your mind, within 24 hours after you leave the interview. Include the name and position of the interviewer(s), information about the job (duties, salary) – anything pertinent to the position, your qualifications for the position which you stressed in the interview, and any other information you may need later.

You will have a summary of the interview that you can review prior to a future interview with the firm – whether a follow-up interview for this same position or another opening at a later time.

*   *   *

If you put all of these interview tips into practice, you will be in an excellent position to get the job. You will approach the interview with confidence, energy, and enthusiasm. You will impress the interviewer as someone he or she would like to have working in the organization.

11

Follow-Up and Follow-Through Tips

FOLLOW-UP AND FOLLOW-THROUGH are two of the most important yet neglected job search activities. Taking action that produces results requires some form of follow-up activity. This is especially true when sending resumes and letters, networking, and interviewing for a job. The truth is that most people you target in your job search are very busy people who often have little time to read your resume and letter and seriously consider you for the job. Consequently, it's up to you to make sure you have their attention and stand out from the crowd as a unique and compelling candidate. You do this by engaging in several follow-up activities that help move your candidacy from "inactive" and "under consideration" status to "active" and "under serious consideration" status.

The most effective follow-up and follow-through activities involve sending emails, mailing thank-you letters, and making phone calls. They require setting the stage by indicating to your targeted audience that you will be following up with them in the near future. The tips in this chapter should help point you in the right direction for getting the attention of prospective employers as well as moving them to action favorable to your candidacy.

TIP #132
Be sure to follow up.

Follow-up is a much neglected art, but it is the key to unlocking employers' doors and for achieving job search success. But many people fear following up. Like giving a speech, it requires initiating face-to-face communications with strangers! They would rather mail resumes and wait for a response by email, mail, or telephone.

Follow-up occurs at the implementation stage of your job search. It is the single most important element for converting communications into action. Without an effective follow-up campaign, your letters and resumes will lose their impact. They will probably sit on someone's desk amidst numerous other letters and resumes. If you want your resumes and letters to move readers to take actions that eventually lead to job interviews and offers, you **must** engage in a series of follow-up activities that will give your resumes and letters their intended impact. If you want interviewers to know that you are interested in their position and restate your strongest talents, you need to follow up with a nice thank-you letter and/or phone call.

TIP #133
Develop an effective follow-up system.

Getting your resume and letters read and reacted to and your candidacy remembered are the three most important outcomes you should seek at the pre-interview stage of your job search. You get read, reacted to, and remembered when you follow up with a telephone call and thank-you letter.

Four follow-up principles apply to both resumes and job search letters:

1. **Develop a 31-day follow-up filing system:** Your follow-up activities will quickly become chaotic if you do not develop an efficient and effective management system for handling your communications. While you may want to use an electronic management system (see TIP #88 on pages 136-137), we recommend creating an old-fashioned 31-day filing system. Ideally, this should consist of 31

hanging folders (8½" x 11") labeled numerically by each day of the month (1 thru 31); use manila folders or an expandable file folder if you lack an appropriate filing cabinet or box. Once you communicate with an individual, take a copy of your correspondence – complete with a telephone number and appropriate notes – and place it in the folder with the date (ideally seven days from today) in which you plan to make your next follow-up contact. Repeat this filing activity for all communication requiring a follow-up action. Each day, pull the file for that date and conduct your follow-up actions. If you make a phone call and are unable to contact the person, move a copy of your correspondence to tomorrow's file and conduct another follow-up. Within a month you will have a very efficient and effective filing system that will enable you to systematically conduct follow-ups in a timely and organized manner. Better still, you will be pleasantly surprised to discover this basic filing system produces remarkable results! If you prefer using a computer program for tracking your contacts, try the latest version of ACT! (for information, see www. act.com) or use the automated tracking and record-keeping programs identified on page 137.

2. **Follow up your resume and letters within seven days of mailing them:** Do not let too much time lapse between when you mailed your resume and when you contact the recipient. Seven days should give the recipient sufficient time to examine your communication and decide on your future status. If not, your follow-up actions may assist them in making a decision.

3. **The best follow-up for a mailed resume and letter is a telephone call:** Don't expect your resume recipient to take the initiative in calling you for an interview. State in your cover letter that you will call the recipient at a particular time to discuss your resume:

> *"I will call your office on the morning of November 5 to see if a meeting can be scheduled at a convenient time."*

And be sure you indeed follow up with a phone call at the designated time. If you have difficulty contacting the individual, try no more than eight times to get through. After the eighth try, leave a message as well as write a letter as an alternative to the telephone follow-up. In this letter, inquire about the status of your resume and thank the individual for his or her consideration.

4. **Follow up your follow- up with a nice thank-you letter:** Regardless of the outcome of your phone call, send a nice thank-you letter based upon your conversation. You thank the recipient for taking the time to speak with you and reiterate your interest in the position.

TIP #134
Send thank-you letters.

As soon as possible after the interview – later the same day or the next day at the latest – send a thank-you letter. In this letter express your appreciation for the time the interviewer(s) spent with you, indicate your continued interest in the position (if this is the case), and restate any special skills or experience you would bring to the job (keep this brief and well focused). This is a business letter and the stationery, format, and writing style should reflect your professionalism. For examples of numerous such effective letters, see our companion volumes, *201 Dynamite Job Search Letters* and *Nail the Cover Letter!* (Impact Publications).

TIP #135
Be pleasant and persistent when you follow up.

Always close your letters with a follow-up statement rather than the standard but rather limp *"I look forward to hearing from you"* close. Try to end with a closing that uses some variation of these follow-up statements:

"I will call your office on Tuesday, February 5, to see if your schedule would permit us to meet briefly."

"I know you're very busy. But I also know I could benefit greatly from your advice. I would like to call you on Thursday morning to briefly discuss my interests. I'll only take a few minutes of your time."

"I will call your office at 2pm on Thursday, April 23, to ask you a few questions about my interests and to see if we might be able to get together for a brief meeting in the near future."

"Would next week be a good time to discuss my interests? I'll call your office at 3pm on Tuesday, September 9, to check your schedule. I appreciate your time."

Each of these statements specifies **what** you will do and **when** you plan to do it – an anticipated follow-up action on your part. The reader knows what to expect next from you. At this stage he or she needs to do nothing other than **remember** you and your letter – the most important outcome you want to achieve when initially developing a communication link with your reader.

Conducting an effective follow-up by telephone is easier said than done, especially given today's frustrating voice mail systems (although see Neil McNulty's terrific voice mail tips in *The Quick 30/30 Job Solution* for turning voice mail to your advantage). A typical follow-up may require three to seven phone calls because the person is unavailable or avoiding your call. With each phone call you may need to leave a message. However, similar to response rates to letters, don't expect busy people to return phone calls from strangers. Many people only do so after the third or fourth redundant phone message – guilt moves them to action!

Whatever you do, don't show your irritation, anger, or disappointment in not having your calls returned. Some people feel insulted and express their irritation in their tone of voice or choice of words when they make their third, fourth, or fifth ineffective follow-up call:

"Well, I left two messages – one on Tuesday and another on Wednesday."

"Does he usually return his phone calls?"

"What should I do? I keep calling but he won't return my calls!"

"Did he leave a message for me?"

"How many more days should I wait before I call again?"

These responses communicate the wrong **attitude** toward someone who may be able to assist you. While they may accurately reflect what is happening, they lack tact and good job search manners. Keep your cool, and cheerfully keep leaving messages as if you understand this is what normally happens in the course of conducting follow-up calls. Remember, you are sowing the seeds of what will probably be a guilt-felt and sympathetic individual who eventually, and apologetically, returns your calls.

A standard follow-up scenario goes something like this. You stated in your letter you would call at 2:30pm on Tuesday. When you call, you will probably have to go through one or two gatekeepers before you can make direct contact with the person you want to reach. The final gatekeeper will probably be a personal secretary or receptionist who is well versed in the art of screening important from not-so-important calls. When the final gatekeeper takes your call, the following exchange is likely to occur:

SECRETARY: *"Mr. Carroll's office. How can I help you?"*

YOU: *"Hi, this is Mary Harris calling for Mr. Carroll."*

SECRETARY: *"I'm sorry, Mr. Carroll is not available."*

YOU: *"When would you expect him to be free?"*

SECRETARY: *"I really don't know. He's been in meetings all day. Could I take a message and have him return your call?"*

YOU: *"Yes, would you please? My name is Mary Harris and my telephone number is _____. I'm calling in reference to a letter I sent Mr. Carroll on July 5. I mentioned I would be calling him today."*

SECRETARY: *"I'll give him the message."*

YOU: *"Thanks so much for your help."*

Don't hold your breath in expectation of getting a return call soon. The secretary will give him the message, but he probably will sit on it and do nothing until he's motivated to do so. Consequently, you will probably need to initiate another call. If you don't hear from him within 24 hours, make another follow-up call. This time your conversation may go something like this:

SECRETARY:	_"Mr. Carroll's office. How can I help you?"_
YOU:	_"Hi, this is Mary Harris calling for Mr. Carroll."_
SECRETARY:	_"I'm sorry, Mr. Carroll is not available. Can I take a message?"_
YOU:	_"Yes. Can you tell him Mary Harris called. My telephone number is _____. I'm calling in reference to my letter of July 5. I also called yesterday and left a message."_
SECRETARY:	_"Oh, yes. I remember your call. I did give him the message. However, he's been extremely busy. I'll make sure he gets the message again."_

You may get a return call, but don't hold your breath. You will probably need to initiate another call or two before you make direct contact. Again, wait 24 hours to call again. With a third call you will most likely have the attention of both the secretary and the letter recipient. Both may start to feel somewhat guilty for not taking your call. The secretary especially feels responsible because she obviously has been ineffective vis-a-vis both you and her boss. The letter recipient is beginning to collect a pile of message notes indicating the same person is waiting for a return call. At this point the secretary is likely to make certain decisions: the next time you call, she will make a special effort to remind her boss that you have called several times, and it would be nice to return the call or give a more hopeful response than _"I'll give him the message"_; or she will ask her boss if she should relay any special message to Mary Harris should she call again. Your fourth follow-up call may result in a change in dialogue:

SECRETARY:	_"Mr. Carroll's office. How can I help you?"_
YOU:	_"Hi, this is Mary Harris calling for Mr. Carroll."_

SECRETARY: *"Yes, I remember you called earlier. I'm sorry Mr.
Carroll hasn't been able to get back with you. He's
been so busy. When I spoke with him yesterday, he
said he would call you today around 4pm."*

Making several follow-up phone calls demonstrates your persistence. While it's unfortunate you may have to make so many calls, especially if they are expensive long-distance calls, that's the reality of communicating in today's busy business world. Such persistence eventually pays off because you become **remembered** and because many individuals **feel guilty** about not returning your calls after receiving the same message over and over again from the same person.

> *Persistence pays off because you become remembered and because many people feel guilty not returning your calls.*

You might also try to follow up by email. However, many employers have two emails – one public and one private. You need to direct your email to the private one (see *The Quick 30/30 Job Solution* for tips on how to do this). Many people treat email from strangers as junk mail – an unwelcome intrusion into their lives worthy of a quick delete. Don't expect to increase your response rate, nor the quality of your response, by resorting to impersonal email. In fact, many people resent having what they consider to be a private channel of communications – their email – invaded by strangers

TIP #136
Follow up your follow-up.

Once you make telephone contact, be sure to follow up this follow-up call with a nice thank-you letter. Again, your goal is not just to get useful job information. Your goal should also include being **remembered** for future reference. You want busy people to remember you, because they are likely to refer you to other busy people who may be looking for individuals with your qualifications. In other words, the thank-you follow-up letter becomes an important building block for expanding your network for information, advice, and referrals. Job seekers who follow up their follow-up calls with a thank-you letter are more likely to be remembered than those who merely hang up the phone and move on to other follow-up calls.

TIP #137
Do what you say you will do when setting a call time.

It's funny what you learn about people through their letters. Today more and more job seekers close their letters with an effective follow-up statement, but they never follow up. They simply don't do what they say they will! Indeed, the last three letters I received from job seekers included the date and time they would call me to follow up. They wrote nice letters – modeled after the advice of "how-to" job search letter books – but I have yet to hear from them. Somewhere along the way to the mailbox no one told them they actually had to follow up their letter! Yes, I remember these people, but unfortunately I remember them for what they did to me – wasted my time with a canned follow-up statement they had no intention of doing anything about.

Many job seekers say in their letters that they will follow up at a particular time but they never do.

Whatever you do, make sure your letters represent **you**. Moreover, make sure you **do** exactly what you say you will do. If you tell your reader you will call them at 2:30 on Thursday afternoon, make sure you call exactly at that time. The person may have penciled in this time on his calendar to speak with you. If you fail to do so, the individual is likely to remember you in negative terms – this job seeker doesn't follow through or keep appointments! You'll have difficulty recovering from such an initial negative impression. You will be wasting both your time and the time of the reader.

TIP #138
Follow through with a telephone call when the decision date has passed.

Remember (Tip #126) at the end of the interview you asked when a decision would be made, and asked whether you could call if you hadn't heard within a couple of days of that date? Don't just ask the question and leave it at that – you must follow through. If the decision date has passed you **must** make the follow-up call.

If no decision has yet been made, your call will remind them of your continued interest. You also should impress the employer as someone who does follow through, and he could expect this same commitment from you as an employee. If the employer has made a decision and was about to call and offer you the position, that's great! If someone else has been offered the job you may be disappointed, but it is just as well to find out now and concentrate your job search efforts elsewhere than to waste time waiting to hear about this job.

TIP #139
Evaluate your follow-up competencies.

Let's evaluate the potential effectiveness of your implementation and follow-up activities. Respond to each of the these statements by indicating how you dealt with each follow-up action:

Follow-Up Actions	Yes	No
1. Completed the "Job Search Contract." (See Tip #4)	1	3
2. Completed my first "Weekly Job Search Performance and Planning Report." (See Tip #4)	1	3
3. Ended my letter with an action statement indicating I would contact the individual by phone within the next week.	1	3
4. Made the first follow-up call at the time and date indicated in my letter.	1	3

5. Followed up with additional phone calls until I was able to speak directly with the person or received the requested information.   1   3

6. Maintained a positive and professional attitude during each follow-up activity. Was pleasantly persistent and tactful during all follow-up calls. Never indicated I was irritated, insulted, or disappointed in not having my phone calls returned.   1   3

7. Followed up the follow-up by sending a thank-you letter genuinely expressing my appreciation for the person's time and information.   1   3

TOTAL

Add the numbers you circled to the right of each statement to get a cumulative score. If your score is higher than 7, you need to work on improving the effectiveness of your implementation and follow-up competencies. Go back and institute the necessary changes in your implementation and follow-up behavior so your next resumes and letters will be a perfect 7!

12

Salary Negotiation
and Job Offer Tips

I N THE END, YOU WANT to be fairly compensated for your
talent. However, many job seekers make several salary mistakes,
from not knowing their worth and prematurely discussing salary
to failing to properly negotiate a compensation package that truly
reflects their value in today's job market. Part of the problem is
cultural – reluctance to talk about money and other people's salaries.
But the major problem relates to the lack of compensation information
and salary negotiation skills.

The tips in this chapter introduce you to the major issues relating
to salary and job offers. For more information on how to become a
savvy salary negotiator, see my three companion volumes: *Give Me
More Money!*, *Salary Negotiation Tips for Professionals*, and *Get
a Raise in 7 Days* (Impact Publications).

TIP #140
Most salaries are negotiable.

Contrary to what many job seekers believe, salary is seldom predeter-
mined. Most employers have some flexibility to negotiate salary or
benefits. While most employers do not try to exploit applicants,

neither do they want to pay applicants more than what they have to or what a candidate will accept. Salaries for entry-level jobs usually are the least flexible. There may be little room for negotiation if you are applying for an entry-level job or have no record of accomplishments.

Salaries are usually assigned to positions or jobs rather than to individuals. But not everyone is of equal value in performing the job; some are more productive than others. Since individual performance differs, you should attempt to establish your value in the eyes of the employer rather than accept a salary figure for the job. The art of salary negotiation will help you do this.

TIP #141
Become a savvy salary negotiator.

Just how savvy a salary negotiator are you? How prepared are you to negotiate a salary that truly reflects your worth? What knowledge and skills do you need to become a savvy salary negotiator?

Let's start by evaluating your knowledge and skill level for becoming an effective salary negotiator. Respond to the following statements by circling "Yes" or "No." If you are uncertain about your answer, just leave the statement alone and move on to the next statement.

1. I know what I'm worth in comparison
    to others in today's job market.   Yes   No

2. I know what others make in my company.   Yes   No

3. I can negotiate a salary 15 percent higher
    than my current salary.   Yes   No

4. I can negotiate a salary 5-10 percent higher
    than what the employer is prepared to offer me. Yes   No

5. I know where I can quicky find salary
    information for my particular position.   Yes   No

6. I usually feel comfortable talking about
    compensation issues with others, including
    my boss.   Yes   No

7. I'm familiar with how various compensation
    options work with most employers, such as

	signing bonuses, performance bonuses, cafeteria plans, reimbursement accounts, disability insurance, 401(k) plans, SEPs, CODAs, stock options, flex-time, tuition reimbursements, and severance pay.	Yes	No
8.	I understand the different types of stock options and equity incentives offered by employers in my field.	Yes	No
9.	I know what my current compensation package is worth when translated into dollar equivalents.	Yes	No
10.	I'm prepared to negotiate more than seven different compensation options.	Yes	No
11.	I have a list of at least 50 accomplishments and a clear pattern of performance which I can communicate to prospective employers.	Yes	No
12.	I'm prepared to tell at least five different one- to three-minute stories about my proudest achievements.	Yes	No
13.	If asked to state my "salary requirements" in a cover letter or on an application, I know what to write.	Yes	No
14.	I know when I should and should not discuss salary during an interview.	Yes	No
15.	I know what to best say if the interviewer asks me *"What are your salary expectations?"*	Yes	No
16.	I know what questions to ask during the interview in order to get information about salaries in the interviewer's company.	Yes	No
17.	I know when it's time to stop talking and start serious negotiations.	Yes	No
18.	I know how to use the "salary range" to create "common ground" and strengthen my negotiation position.	Yes	No

19. I know how to use silence to strengthen
     my negotiation position.   Yes   No

20. If offered a position, I know what to
     say and do next.   Yes   No

If you responded "No" to more than three of the above statements or "Yes" to fewer than 15 of the statements, you need to work on developing your salary negotiation skills.

TIP #142
Avoid 21 salary negotiation mistakes

Job seekers typically make several salary negotiation errors, which often result in knocking them out of consideration for the job or receiving and accepting a lower salary offer than what they could have received had they practiced a few of the salary tips outlined in this chapter. Several of these errors also may leave a bad impression with an employer – that you have a bad attitude, or you are basically a self-centered job seeker who primarily focuses on salary and benefits rather than on the performance needs of the employer and organization. The most frequent errors you should avoid include:

1. Engaging in wishful thinking – believing you are worth a lot more than you are currently being paid but having no credible evidence of what you really should be paid.

2. Approaching the job search as an exercise in being clever and manipulative rather than being clear, correct, and competent in communicating your value to others.

3. Failing to research salary options and comparables and thus having few supports to justify your worth.

4. Fail to compile a list of specific accomplishments, including anecdotal one- to three-minute performance stories, that provide evidence of your value to employers.

5. Revealing salary expectations on the resume or in a letter.

6. Answering the question *"What are your salary requirements?"* before being offered the job.

7. Raising the salary question rather than waiting for the employer to do so.

8. Failing to ask questions about the company, job, and previous occupants of the position.

9. Asking *"Is this offer negotiable?"*

10. Quickly accepting the first offer, believing that's what the position is really worth and that an employer might be offended if one tries to negotiate.

11. Accepting the offer on the spot.

12. Accepting the offer primarily because of compensation.

13. Trying to negotiate compensation during the first interview.

14. Forgetting to calculate the value of benefits and thus only focusing on the gross salary figure.

15. Focusing on benefits, stock options, and perks rather than on the gross salary figure.

16. Negotiating a salary figure rather discussing a salary range.

17. Negotiating over the telephone or by email.

18. Talking too much and listening too little.

19. Focusing on your needs rather than the employer's needs.

20. Trying to play "hardball."

21. Expressing a negative attitude toward the employer's offer.

TIP #143
Avoid discussing salary before being offered the job.

Employers often raise the salary question early in the interview. They may actually do this during a telephone screening interview. Their basic goal is to either screen you into or out of consideration for the position on salary criteria. Like stating your salary expectations on a resume or in a cover letter, responding to this question with a figure early in the interview puts you at a disadvantage. The old poker saying that _"He who reveals his hand first is at a disadvantage"_ is especially true when negotiating salary. Time should work in your favor. After all, you need more information about the job and your responsibilities in order to determine the value of the position. What is the job really worth? A $60,000 a year

> _Salary should be the very last thing you talk about – **after** you receive a job offer._

job has different levels of responsibility than one worth only $30,000 a year. If the employer raises the salary expectation question early in the interview, it's best to respond by saying _"I really need to know more about the position and my responsibilities before I can discuss compensation. Can you tell me about . . . ?"_ This response will usually result in postponing the salary question and impress upon the employer that you are a thoughtful professional who is more employer-centered than self-centered with your interest in the position. Salary should be the very last thing you talk about – within the context of a job offer, which may be after two or three interviews. Once you have been offered the job, then talk about compensation.

TIP #144
Let the employer volunteer salary information.

Today, many candidates go through three to seven interviews with an employer before receiving a job offer. The first interview seldom deals with the money question, although this question can arise at anytime to screen someone into or out of consideration. You should never raise the salary issue, for to do so puts you at a disadvantage. Expect the salary offer, and accompanying salary negotiations, to take place during the **final** interview. The sign of when you should talk seriously about money is when you are offered the job. The offer comes first followed by discussion of appropriate compensation. Another way of handling the *"What are your salary requirements?"* question is to respond by asking *"Are you offering me the position?"* If the response is *"No,"* then you might respond by saying *"I really need to know more about the position and your company before I feel comfortable discussing compensation."* Alternatively, you might want to use this occasion to do research on the company's salary structure by asking *"By the way, how much are you paying at present for this position?"* Always try to get the employer to volunteer salary information from which you can formulate your response.

TIP #145
Look at the total compensation package.

One of the easiest ways to survey your compensation options and assign value to your ideal compensation package is to use the following checklist of compensation options. Consider each item and then value it by assigning a dollar amount. When finished, add up the total dollars assigned to get a complete picture of the value of your present or past compensation package.

Element	Value

Basic Compensation Issues

❏ Base salary $ _____
❏ Commissions $ _____
❏ Corporate profit sharing $ _____
❏ Personal performance bonuses/incentives $ _____
❏ Cost of living adjustment $ _____
❏ Overtime $ _____
❏ Signing bonus $ _____
❏ Cash in lieu of certain benefits $ _____

Health Benefits

- ❏ Medical insurance $ _____
- ❏ Dental insurance $ _____
- ❏ Vision insurance $ _____
- ❏ Prescription package $ _____
- ❏ Life insurance $ _____
- ❏ Accidental death and disability insurance $ _____
- ❏ Evacuation insurance (international travel) $ _____

Vacation and Time Issues

- ❏ Vacation time $ _____
- ❏ Sick days $ _____
- ❏ Personal time $ _____
- ❏ Holidays $ _____
- ❏ Flex-time $ _____
- ❏ Compensatory time $ _____
- ❏ Paternity/maternity leave $ _____
- ❏ Family leave $ _____

Retirement-Oriented Benefits

- ❏ Defined benefit plan $ _____
- ❏ 401(k) plan $ _____
- ❏ Deferred compensation $ _____
- ❏ Savings plans $ _____
- ❏ Stock-purchase plans $ _____
- ❏ Stock bonus $ _____
- ❏ Stock options $ _____
- ❏ Ownership/equity $ _____

Education

- ❏ Professional continuing education $ _____
- ❏ Tuition reimbursement for you or your family members $ _____

Military

- ❏ Compensatory pay during active duty $ _____
- ❏ National Guard $ _____

Perquisites

- ❏ Cellular phone $ _____
- ❏ Company car or vehicle/mileage allowance $ _____
- ❏ Expense accounts $ _____

❑ Liberalization of business-related expenses $ _____
❑ Child care $ _____
❑ Cafeteria privileges $ _____
❑ Executive dining room privileges $ _____
❑ First-class hotels $ _____
❑ First-class air travel $ _____
❑ Upgrade business travel $ _____
❑ Personal use of frequent-flyer awards $ _____
❑ Convention participation: professionally related $ _____
❑ Parking $ _____
❑ Paid travel for spouse $ _____
❑ Professional association memberships $ _____
❑ Athletic club memberships $ _____
❑ Social club memberships $ _____
❑ Use of company-owned facilities $ _____
❑ Executive office $ _____
❑ Office with a window $ _____
❑ Laptop computers $ _____
❑ Private secretary $ _____
❑ Portable fax $ _____
❑ Employee discounts $ _____
❑ Incentive trips $ _____
❑ Sabbaticals $ _____
❑ Discounted buying club memberships $ _____
❑ Free drinks and meals $ _____

Relocation Expenses

❑ Direct moving expenses $ _____
❑ Moving costs for unusual property $ _____
❑ Trips to find suitable housing $ _____
❑ Loss on sale of present home
　　or lease termination $ _____
❑ Company handling sale of present home $ _____
❑ Housing cost differential between cities $ _____
❑ Mortgage rate differential $ _____
❑ Mortgage fees and closing costs $ _____
❑ Temporary dual housing $ _____
❑ Trips home during dual residency $ _____
❑ Real estate fees $ _____
❑ Utilities hookup $ _____
❑ Drapes/carpets $ _____
❑ Appliance installation $ _____
❑ Auto/pet shipping $ _____
❑ Signing bonus for incidental expenses $ _____
❑ Additional meals expense account $ _____

❑ Bridge loan while owning two homes $ _____
❑ Outplacement assistance for spouse $ _____

Home Office Options

❑ Personal computer $ _____
❑ Internet access $ _____
❑ Copier $ _____
❑ Printer $ _____
❑ Financial planning assistance $ _____
❑ Separate phone line $ _____
❑ Separate fax line $ _____
❑ CPA/tax assistance $ _____
❑ Incidental/support office functions $ _____
❑ Office supplies $ _____
❑ Furniture and accessories $ _____

Severance Packages (Parachutes)

❑ Base salary $ _____
❑ Bonuses/incentives $ _____
❑ Non-compete clause $ _____
❑ Stock/equity $ _____
❑ Outplacement assistance $ _____
❑ Voice mail access $ _____
❑ Statement (letter) explaining why you left $ _____
❑ Vacation reimbursement $ _____
❑ Health benefits or reimbursements $ _____
❑ 401(k) contributions $ _____

TOTAL $ _____

TIP #146
Focus on salary ranges.

Savvy salary negotiators always talk about "salary ranges" rather than specific salary figures. They do so because ranges give them flexibility in the negotiation process. If, for example, the employer reveals his hand first by saying the job pays $60,000 a year, you should counter by putting the employer's figure at the bottom of your range – *"Based on my salary research as well as my experience, I was thinking more in terms of $60,000 to $70,000 a year."* By doing this, you establish common ground from which to negotiate the figure upwards toward the high end of your range. While the employer may not want to pay more than $60,000, he or she at least knows you are within budget. The employer most likely will counter by saying, *"Well, we might be able to go $63,000."* You, in turn, can counter by saying *"Is it possible to go $66,000?"* As you will quickly discover in the salary negotiation business, anything is "possible" if you handle the situation profes-sionally – with supports and flexi-bility. In this situation, you might have been able to negotiate a $6,000 increase over the employ-er's initial offer because you estab-lished common ground with a salary range and then moved the employer toward the upper end of your range because you had sup-ports and professional appeal.

> *Establish common ground from which to negotiate the figure upwards toward the high end of your range.*

TIP #147
Carefully examine benefits.

Many employers will try to impress candidates with the benefits offered by the company. These might include retirement, bonuses, stock options, medical and life insurance, and cost of living adjust-ments. If the employer includes these benefits in the salary negotia-tions, do not be overly impressed. Most benefits are standard – they come with the job. When negotiating salary, it is best to talk about specific dollar figures. But don't neglect to both calculate and nego-tiate benefits according to the checklist on pages 212-215. Benefits can translate into a significant portion of your compensation, espe-cially if you are offered stock options, profit sharing, pensions, in-surance, and reimbursement accounts. Indeed, many individuals in the 1990s who took stock options in lieu of high salaries with start-up high-tech firms discovered the importance of benefits when their benefits far outweighed their salaries; making only $30,000 a year, some of them became instant millionaires when their companies went public! In fact, the U.S. Department of Labor estimates that benefits now constitute 43 percent of total compensation for the average worker. For example, a $60,000 offer with Company X may translate into a compensation package worth $80,000, but a $50,000 offer with Company Y may actually be worth more than $100,000 when you examine their different benefits.

If the salary offered by the employer does not meet your expectations, but you still want the job, you might try to negotiate for some benefits which are not considered standard. These might include longer paid vacations, some flex-time, and profit sharing.

TIP #148
Avoid playing hard-to-get and other unprofessional games.

If you get a job offer but you are considering other employers, let the others know you have a job offer. Telephone them to inquire about your status as well as inform them of the job offer. Sometimes this will prompt employers to make a hiring decision sooner than anticipated. In addition you will be informing them that you are in demand; they should seriously consider you before you get away!

Some job seekers play a bluffing game by telling employers they have alternative job offers even though they don't. Some candidates do this and get away with it. We don't recommend this approach. Not only is it dishonest, it will work to your disadvantage if the employer learns that you were lying. But more important, you should be selling yourself on the basis of your strengths rather than your deceit and greed. If you can't sell yourself honestly, don't expect to get along well on the job. When you compromise your integrity, you demean your value to others and yourself.

TIP #149
Delay accepting an offer until you've had a chance to seriously consider it.

You should accept an offer only after reaching a salary agreement. If you jump at an offer, you may appear needy. Take time to consider your options. Remember, you are committing your time and effort in exchange for money and status. Is this the job you really want? Take some time to think about the offer before giving the employer a definite answer. But don't play hard-to-get and thereby create ill-will with your new employer.

While considering the offer, ask yourself several of the same questions you asked at the beginning of your job search:

- What do I want to be doing five years from now?

- How will this job affect my personal life?

- Do I want to travel?

- Do I know enough about the employer and the future of this organization?

- How have previous occupants of this position fared? Why did they have problems?

- Are there other job opportunities that would better meet my goals?

Accepting a job is serious business. If you make a mistake, you could be locked into a very unhappy situation for a long time.

If you receive one job offer while considering another, you will be able to compare relative advantages and disadvantages. You also will have some external leverage for negotiating salary and benefits. While you should not play games, let the employer know you have alternative job offers. This communicates that you are in demand, others also know your value, and the employer's price is not the only one in town. Use this leverage to negotiate your salary, benefits, and job responsibilities.

TIP #150
Get the job offer in writing.

You should take notes throughout the salary negotiation session. Jot down pertinent information about the terms of employment. At the end of the session, before you get up to leave, summarize what you understand will be included in the compensation package and show it in outline form to the employer. Make sure both you and the employer understand the terms of employment, including specific elements in the compensation package. If you accept the position, be sure to ask the employer to put the offer in writing, which may be in the form of a letter of agreement. This document should spell out your duties and responsibilities as well as detail how you will be compensated. If your agreement includes incentivized pay, make sure it details exactly how your commissions or bonuses will work – how and when they will be paid, set up, and measured. For example, will you be paid at the end of each quarter or at the end of the year? Do you receive a flat bonus, such as $1,000, or a percentage of the sales from an income stream.

Ask the employer to email or fax you a copy of this document for your review. Let him know you'll get back with him immediately. This document should serve as your employment contract.

The Author

F OR MORE THAN TWO DECADES Ron Krannich, Ph.D, have pursued a passion – assisting hundreds of thousands of individuals, from students, the unemployed, and ex-offenders to military personnel, international job seekers, and CEOs, in making critical job and career transitions. Focusing on key job search skills, career changes, and employment fields, his impressive body of work has helped shape career thinking and behavior both in the United States and abroad. His sound advice has changed numerous lives, including his own!

Ron is one of America's leading career and travel writers who has authored, co-authored, or ghost-written more than 80 books. A former Peace Corps Volunteer and Fulbright Scholar, Ron received his Ph.D. in Political Science from Northern Illinois University. He operates Development Concepts Incorporated, a training, consulting, and publishing firm in Virginia.

Ron is a former university professor, high school teacher, management trainer, and consultant. As a trainer and consultant, he has completed numerous projects on management, career development, local government, population planning, and rural development in the United States and abroad. His career books focus on key job search skills, military and civilian career transitions, ex-offender re-entry, government and international careers, travel jobs, and nonprofit organizations and include such classics as *High Impact Resumes and Letters, Interview for Success*, and *Change Your Job, Change Your Life*. His books represent one of today's most comprehensive collections of career writing. With over 3 million copies in print, his publications are widely available in bookstores, libraries, and career centers. No stranger to the Internet world, Ron has written *America's Top Internet Job Sites* and *The Directory of Websites for International Jobs* and published several Internet recruitment and job search books. He also have developed career-related websites: www.impactpublications.com, www.exoffenderreentry.com, and www.veteransworld.com. Many of Ron's career tips have appeared on such major websites as www.monster.com, www.careerbuilder.com, www.employmentguide. com, and www.campuscareercenter.com.

Ron lives a double life with travel being his best kept *"do what you love"* career secret. Author of over 20 travel-shopping guidebooks on various destinations around the world, he continues to pursue his international and travel interests through his innovative *Treasures and Pleasures of...Best of the Best* travel-shopping series and *Great Water Destinations* series and related websites: www.ishoparound theworld.com and www.greatwaterdestinations.com. When not found at his home and business in Virginia, he is probably somewhere in Europe, Asia, Africa, the Middle East, the South Pacific, the Caribbean, or the Americas following his other passion – researching and writing about quality antiques, arts, crafts, jewelry, sailing, cruising, beaches, hotels, and restaurants as well as adhering to the career advice he gives to others: *"Pursue a passion that enables you to do what you really love to do."*

Ron's work is frequently featured in major newspapers, magazines, and newsletters as well as on radio, television, and the Internet. Available for interviews, consultation, and presentations – as both a career and travel expert – he can be contacted as follows:

krannich@impactpublications.com

Career Resources

THE FOLLOWING CAREER resources are available directly from Impact Publications. Full descriptions of each title as well as downloadable catalogs, DVDs, software, games, posters, and related products can be found at www.impactpublications.com. Complete this form or list the titles, include shipping (see formula at the end), enclose payment, and send your order to:

IMPACT PUBLICATIONS
9104 Manassas Drive, Suite N
Manassas Park, VA 20111-5211 USA
1-800-361-1055 (orders only)
Tel. 703-361-7300 or Fax 703-335-9486
Email address: query@impactpublications.com
Quick & easy online ordering: www.impactpublications.com

Orders from individuals must be prepaid by check, money order, or major credit card. We accept telephone, fax, and email orders.

Qty.	TITLES	Price	TOTAL
Featured Titles			
____	Job Hunting Tips for People With Hot and Not-So-Hot Backgrounds	$17.95	____
____	Quick Job Finding Pocket Guide	2.95	____
Career Exploration and Job Strategies			
____	40 Best Fields for Your Career	16.95	____
____	50 Best Jobs for Your Personality	17.95	____
____	95 Mistakes Job Seekers Make and How to Avoid Them	13.95	____
____	100 Great Jobs and How to Get Them	17.95	____
____	225 Best Jobs for Baby Boomers	16.95	____
____	250 Best Jobs Through Apprenticeships	24.95	____
____	300 Best Jobs Without a Four-Year Degree	16.95	____
____	About.com Guide to Job Searching	17.95	____
____	America's Top Jobs for People Re-Entering the Workforce	19.95	____

_____	Best Jobs for the 21st Century	19.95 _____
_____	Change Your Job, Change Your Life	21.95 _____
_____	Cool Careers for Dummies	19.99 _____
_____	Directory of Executive Recruiters	59.95 _____
_____	Five Secrets to Finding a Job	12.95 _____
_____	How to Get a Job and Keep It	16.95 _____
_____	How to Succeed Without a Career Path	13.95 _____
_____	Job Hunting Guide: From College to Career	14.95 _____
_____	Knock 'Em Dead	14.95 _____
_____	Me, Myself, and I, Inc.	17.95 _____
_____	No One Is Unemployable	29.95 _____
_____	No One Will Hire Me!	15.95 _____
_____	Occupational Outlook Handbook (annual)	19.95/25.95 _____
_____	O*NET Dictionary of Occupational Titles	39.95/49.95 _____
_____	The Quick 30/30 Job Solution	14.95 _____
_____	Quit Your Job and Grow Some Hair	15.95 _____
_____	Rites of Passage at $100,000 to $1 Million+	29.95 _____
_____	Top 300 Careers	18.95 _____
_____	What Color Is Your Parachute?	18.95 _____

Internet Job Search

_____	America's Top Internet Job Sites	19.95 _____
_____	Best Career and Education Websites	14.95 _____
_____	Directory of Websites for International Jobs	19.95 _____
_____	e-Resumes	16.95 _____
_____	Guide to Internet Job Searching	16.95 _____
_____	Job-Hunting Online	12.95 _____
_____	Job Seeker's Online Goldmine	13.95 _____

Interviews

_____	101 Dynamite Questions to Ask At Your Job Interview	13.95 _____
_____	301 Smart Answers to Tough Interview Questions	12.95 _____
_____	Adams Job Interview Almanac	17.95 _____
_____	Best Answers to 202 Job Interview Questions	17.95 _____
_____	Everything Practice Interview Book	12.95 _____
_____	Ex-Offender's Job Interview Guide	9.95 _____
_____	High-Impact Interview Questions	17.95 _____
_____	I Can't Believe They Asked Me That!	17.95 _____
_____	Interview Magic	18.95 _____
_____	Job Interview Tips for People With Not-So-Hot Backgrounds	14.95 _____
_____	Job Interviews for Dummies	16.99 _____
_____	KeyWords to Nail Your Job Interview	17.95 _____
_____	Nail the Job Interview!	14.95 _____
_____	Perfect Phrases for the Perfect Interview	9.95 _____
_____	The Savvy Interviewer	10.95 _____
_____	Win the Interview, Win the Job	15.95 _____
_____	Winning Job Interviews	12.99 _____
_____	Winning the Interview Game	12.95 _____
_____	You Should Hire Me!	15.95 _____

Salary Negotiations and Surveys

_____	101 Salary Secrets	12.95 _____
_____	250 Best-Paying Jobs	16.95 _____
_____	American Salaries and Wages Survey	251.00 _____
_____	Get a Raise in 7 Days	14.95 _____
_____	Get More Money on Your Next Job	14.95 _____
_____	Give Me More Money!	17.95 _____
_____	Next-Day Salary Negotiation	8.95 _____
_____	Perfect Phrases for Negotiating Salary and Job Offers	9.95 _____
_____	Salary Facts Handbook	39.95 _____
_____	Salary Negotiation Tips for Professionals	16.95 _____
_____	Secrets of Power Salary Negotiating	13.99 _____
_____	Sweaty Palms	13.95 _____

Attitude and Motivation

_____	100 Ways to Motivate Yourself	14.99 _____
_____	Awaken the Giant Within	16.95 _____
_____	Attitude Is Everything	14.95 _____
_____	Change Your Attitude	16.99 _____
_____	Change Your Thinking, Change Your Life	19.95 _____
_____	Eat That Frog!	15.95 _____
_____	Flight Plan	19.95 _____
_____	Goals!	16.95 _____
_____	Little Gold Book of YES! Attitude	19.99 _____
_____	Reinventing Yourself	18.99 _____
_____	The Secret	23.95 _____
_____	Success Principles	16.95 _____

Inspiration and Empowerment

_____	7 Habits of Highly Effective People	15.95 _____
_____	The 8th Habit	15.00 _____
_____	101 Secrets of Highly Effective Speakers	15.95 _____
_____	Create Your Own Future	24.95 _____
_____	Dream It, Do It	16.95 _____
_____	The Habit Change Workbook	19.95 _____
_____	Life Strategies	13.95 _____
_____	The Magic of Thinking Big	14.00 _____
_____	The Power of Positive Thinking	14.95 _____
_____	Power of Purpose	16.95 _____
_____	The Story of You	19.99 _____
_____	Think Big	12.99 _____
_____	Who Moved My Cheese?	19.95 _____

Testing and Assessment

_____	Career, Aptitude, and Selections Tests	17.95 _____
_____	Career Match	15.00 _____
_____	Discover What You're Best At	14.95 _____
_____	Do What You Are	18.99 _____
_____	Employment Personality Tests Decoded	16.99 _____

_____	The Everything Career Tests Book	12.95	_____
_____	Finding Your Perfect Work	16.95	_____
_____	Go Put Your Strengths to Work	30.00	_____
_____	I Could Do Anything If Only I Knew What It Was	16.00	_____
_____	I Want to Do Something Else,		
	But I'm Not Sure What It Is	15.95	_____
_____	Now, Discover Your Strengths	30.00	_____
_____	Pathfinder	16.00	_____
_____	Smarts: Are You Hardwired for Success?	21.95	_____
_____	StrengthsFinder 2.0	19.95	_____
_____	What Should I Do With My Life?	14.95	_____
_____	What Type Am I?	14.95	_____
_____	What's Your Type of Career?	18.95	_____
_____	Who Do You Think You Are?	18.00	_____

Resumes and Letters

_____	101 Great Tips for a Dynamite Resume	13.95	_____
_____	201 Dynamite Job Search Letters	19.95	_____
_____	Best KeyWords for Resumes, Cover Letters,		
	& Interviews	17.95	_____
_____	Best Resumes and CVs for International Jobs	24.95	_____
_____	Best Resumes for $100,000+ Jobs	24.95	_____
_____	Best Resumes for People Without a Four-Year Degree	19.95	_____
_____	Best Cover Letters for $100,000+ Jobs	24.95	_____
_____	Blue-Collar Resume and Job Hunting Guide	15.95	_____
_____	Competency-Based Resumes	13.99	_____
_____	Cover Letter Magic	16.95	_____
_____	Cover Letters for Dummies	16.99	_____
_____	Cover Letters That Knock 'Em Dead	12.95	_____
_____	Create Your Digital Portfolio	19.95	_____
_____	Directory of Professional Resume Writers	17.95	_____
_____	Expert Resumes for Baby Boomers	16.95	_____
_____	Expert Resumes for Career Changers	16.95	_____
_____	Expert Resumes for Computer and Web Jobs	16.95	_____
_____	Expert Resumes for Managers and Executives	16.95	_____
_____	Expert Resumes for People Returning to Work	16.95	_____
_____	Gallery of Best Cover Letters	18.95	_____
_____	Gallery of Best Resumes	18.95	_____
_____	Haldane's Best Cover Letters for Professionals	15.95	_____
_____	Haldane's Best Resumes for Professionals	15.95	_____
_____	High Impact Resumes and Letters	19.95	_____
_____	Internet Resumes	14.95	_____
_____	Military-to-Civilian Resumes and Letters	21.95	_____
_____	Nail the Cover Letter!	17.95	_____
_____	Nail the Resume!	17.95	_____
_____	No-Nonsense Cover Letters	14.99	_____
_____	No-Nonsense Resumes	14.99	_____
_____	Resume Shortcuts	14.95	_____
_____	Resume, Application, and Letter Tips for People		
	With Hot and Not-So-Hot Backgrounds	17.95	_____
_____	Resumes for Dummies	16.99	_____
_____	Resumes That Knock 'Em Dead	12.95	_____

_____	The Savvy Resume Writer	12.95	_____
_____	Step-By-Step Resumes	19.95	_____
_____	Winning Letters That Overcome Barriers to Employment	17.95	_____
_____	World's Greatest Resumes	14.95	_____

Networking

_____	Endless Referrals	16.95	_____
_____	Fine Art of Small Talk	16.95	_____
_____	Great Connections	11.95	_____
_____	How to Work a Room	14.00	_____
_____	Little Black Book of Connections	19.95	_____
_____	Masters of Networking	18.95	_____
_____	Never Eat Alone	24.95	_____
_____	One Phone Call Away	24.95	_____
_____	Power Networking	14.95	_____
_____	The Savvy Networker	13.95	_____
_____	Work the Pond!	15.95	_____

Dress, Image, and Etiquette

_____	Business Etiquette for Dummies	21.99	_____
_____	Dressing Smart for Men	16.95	_____
_____	Dressing Smart for the New Millennium	15.95	_____
_____	Dressing Smart for Women	16.95	_____
_____	Power Etiquette	15.95	_____

Military in Transition

_____	Expert Resumes for Military-to-Civilian Transition	16.95	_____
_____	Jobs and the Military Spouse	17.95	_____
_____	Military-to-Civilian Resumes and Letters	21.95	_____
_____	Military-to-Civilian Career Transition Guide	14.95	_____
_____	Military Spouse's Complete Guide to Career Success	17.95	_____
_____	Military Transition to Civilian Success	21.95	_____

Ex-Offenders and Re-Entry Success

_____	9 to 5 Beats Ten to Life	20.00	_____
_____	99 Days and a Get Up	9.95	_____
_____	Best Jobs for Ex-Offenders	9.95	_____
_____	Best Resumes and Letters for Ex-Offenders	19.95	_____
_____	Ex-Offender Recovery and Re-Entry Guides	33.95	_____
_____	Ex-Offender's 30/30 Job Solution	9.95	_____
_____	Ex-Offender's Job Hunting Guide	17.95	_____
_____	Ex-Offender's Job Interview Guide	9.95	_____
_____	Ex-Offender's Job Search Companion	11.95	_____
_____	Ex-Offender's Quick Job Hunting Guide	9.95	_____
_____	Ex-Offender's Re-Entry Success Guide	9.95	_____
_____	How to Do Good After Prison	19.95	_____
_____	Interview Skills Survival Guide for Ex-Offenders	12.95	_____
_____	Job Search Survival Guide for Ex-Offenders	12.95	_____

____	Job Smarts and Survival Curriculum	71.95	____
____	Life Without a Crutch	7.95	____
____	Man, I Need a Job	7.95	____

Government and Security Jobs

____	Book of U.S. Government Jobs	22.95	____
____	Complete Guide to Public Employment	19.95	____
____	Federal Applications That Get Results	23.95	____
____	FBI Careers	19.95	____
____	Federal Law Enforcement Careers	19.95	____
____	Post Office Jobs	24.95	____
____	Ten Steps to a Federal Job	28.95	____

SUBTOTAL ____

Virginia residents add 5% sales tax ____

POSTAGE/HANDLING ($5 for first
product and 9% of SUBTOTAL) ____$5.00____

9% of SUBTOTAL --- ____
(Include an additional 15% if shipping outside
the continental United States) ----------------------------- ____

TOTAL ENCLOSED ------------------------ ____

SHIP TO:

NAME _____

ADDRESS _____

_____

_____

PAYMENT METHOD:

❑ I enclose check/money order for $ _____ made payable to
IMPACT PUBLICATIONS.

❑ Please charge $ _____ to my credit card:
❑ Visa   ❑ MasterCard   ❑ American Express   ❑ Discover

Card # _____ Expiration date: ____/____

Signature _____

Your One-Stop Career, Life Skills, and Travel Centers

Books, DVDs, posters, games, pamphlets, and articles on jobs, careers, education, travel, military, ex-offenders, anger management, addiction, recovery, mental health, and much more!

www.impactpublications.com
www.exoffenderreentry.com
www.veteransworld.com
www.ishoparoundtheworld.com